an illustrated introduction to
THE BATTLE OF WATERLOO

Mark Simner

The Battle of Waterloo, Jan Willem Pieneman, 1824. This painting depicts the turning point in the battle.

First published 2015

Amberley Publishing
The Hill, Stroud
Gloucestershire, GL5 4EP

www.amberley-books.com

British Library Cataloguing in Publication Data.
A catalogue record for this book is available from the British Library.

ISBN 978 1 4456 4666 4 (paperback)
ISBN 978 1 4456 4667 1 (ebook)

Typesetting and Origination by Amberley Publishing.
Printed in Great Britain.

CONTENTS

WATERLOO
IN FIVE MINUTES

The Battle of Waterloo marked the end of almost a quarter of a century of conflict which, until the First World War almost 100 years later, was known in the English-speaking world as the 'Great War'. In reality it was not one continuous war, rather a series of conflicts that are referred to today as the French Revolutionary and Napoleonic Wars. These conflicts were not only fought in Europe but across the globe, with many nation states being involved to a greater or lesser degree between 1792 and 1815.

It was the French Revolution that acted as the spark to these conflicts, when in 1789 the people of France rose against the unpopular Louis XVI and overthrew the *Ancien Régime*. Although the causes of the Revolution are both complex and deep-rooted, it is perhaps the policies of the king that finally pushed the people too far. For example, France had fought a number of costly wars against the British, including the Seven Years' War and the American War of Independence, which had left her with huge debts. Louis XVI had supported the Americans in their bid for freedom in the hope they would offer trading rights in return. Yet despite the fact that the British defeat owed much to French help, the Americans continued to trade with their former enemy and gave little to France in return.

The Revolution inherited all the problems of the former government, and a distraction from domestic issues was needed. This was found in the form of war, and Revolutionary France was not short of enemies abroad. Thus began the French Revolutionary Wars fought between 1792 and 1802, conflicts that would spill across western and central Europe, the Middle East, southern Africa and the West Indies. The survival of the Revolution become one and the same as the survival of the nation.

Against this backdrop of revolution and war came opportunities for Napoleon Bonaparte to rise from relative obscurity to be the most powerful man in Europe

Opposite: Vielle Garde à Waterloo, 18 Juin 1815. (Anne S. K. Brown Military Collection, Brown University Library)

(we explore this in more detail in chapter 1). From a family of minor Corsican nobility, Napoleon would quickly demonstrate his incredible military abilities, which would earn him swift promotion, and by 1799 in a *coup d'état* the young general had seized power over France, becoming first consul. Napoleon had effectively ended the bloody Revolution, and although France was in theory still a republic, it had in reality become a dictatorship. The Napoleonic Wars would follow, and in December 1804 the first consul became emperor.

The emperor brought much glory to France, but by 1814 he faced defeat, with his enemies closing in on him from all around. Forced to abdicate, he was sent into exile on the island of Elba, where he was meant to live out his days as ruler of the tiny kingdom. However, ever the opportunist and sensing the moment was right, Napoleon escaped the following year and returned to France, and, in what was a masterstroke, he once again sat on the French throne as emperor (see chapter 2).

Perhaps unsurprisingly, the European powers that had dealt Napoleon defeat only months before were not willing to allow him to remain as ruler. With that they declared war on him personally and set about raising a huge army consisting of Austrian, Russian, Prussian and Anglo-Allied troops. As the Allies conspired to invade France, the newly restored emperor planned to deal a knockout blow to the Prussian and Anglo-Allied armies in the Low Countries while they waited for their Austrian and Russian coalition partners to arrive.

And so began what is known as the Hundred Days, or War of the Seventh Coalition, a conflict that would see four major battles as well as a series of minor skirmishes. Napoleon invaded Belgium on 15 June 1815, his plan being to manoeuvre his army in between his two adversaries before defeating each in turn. On the following day the first two major actions would be fought simultaneously, Michel Ney engaging Wellington's Anglo-Allies at Quatre-Bras while the emperor fought Blücher's Prussians at Ligny. Although victorious at Ligny, Napoleon failed to destroy the Prussian army, which enabled them to conduct a withdrawal north to Wavre, where they regrouped. Blücher was determined to march to Wellington's aid and fight again.

The night before the Battle of Waterloo was a miserable one; heavy rains ensured the men would begin 18 June soaked to the skin and covered in mud. Wellington deployed his army along the ridge of Mont-Saint-Jean, while Napoleon positioned his force on the opposite ridge of La Belle Alliance. Wellington knew he was unlikely to beat the emperor alone with the hotchpotch that was the Anglo-Allied army, but he was relying on Blücher's promise of assistance to secure victory.

Although the actual time is still disputed by historians, the Battle of Waterloo began around 11:30 on 18 June 1815. The action can be split into five phases, although these phases do not always begin when the previous one ends and some continue throughout much of the day. However, the first phase (explored in chapter 3) would include the diversionary attack on the château of Hougoumont, where Jérôme Bonaparte, Napoleon's brother, ordered repeated assaults against the defenders in front of Wellington's right-flank. All would fail, but both sides would be forced to commit an increasing number of men to this 'battle within a battle'.

The second phase (chapter 4) began around 13:30 with the advance of d'Erlon's I Corps against the centre of the Anglo-Allied line, where four of the five demoralised battalions of Bijlandt's mixed Dutch and Belgian brigade failed to hold their section of the line and broke. This opened a 250-metre gap in Wellington's line, but potential defeat was averted by the intervention of the British heavy cavalry, who hacked their way into d'Erlon's divisions. What should have been a British masterstroke then turned to disaster when, with their horses blown, the Household and Union brigades were counter-attacked and heavily mauled by French *cuirassiers* and *lanciers*.

Phase three (chapter 5) included Ney's mistaken belief that Wellington was beginning a withdrawal, and he led charge after charge of French cavalry against the squares of the Anglo-Allied army between 16:00 and 18:00. All failed, but it put Wellington's men under extreme pressure in what would soon become the crisis of the battle. La Haye-Sainte, forward of Wellington's centre, would also fall to the French.

However, the balance would begin to tip in the favour of the Allies when, with phase four (chapter 6), Bülow's Prussian IV Corps finally arrived on the field at around 16:30. After driving back Lobau's French VI Corps, the two armies became involved in a bitter contest for the possession of Plancenoit, which both Blücher and Napoleon knew held the key to victory. The emperor would be forced to divert increasing numbers of precious reserves into the defence of the village.

Finally, in phase five (chapter 7), Napoleon committed his famed Garde Impériale at around 19:30 in a last attempt to smash the Anglo-Allied line. Unfortunately for the emperor, his elite troops failed to secure victory and, after being mauled by Allied artillery and musket fire, were compelled to retire. Seeing this, Wellington ordered a general advance while Blücher's Prussians finally took Plancenoit and began to march on La Belle Alliance. Under this extreme pressure the French army started to disintegrate and flee from the field. The battle was over; Napoleon's last throw of the dice had failed.

TIMELINE

- **26 February 1815**
  Following escape from Elba, Napoleon lands with an army of 1,026 at Golfe-Juan near Antibes and begins his journey to Paris.

- **13 March 1815**
  The Congress of Vienna declares Napoleon an outlaw and declares war on him personally.

- **19/20 March 1815**
  Louis XVIII flees Paris for Ghent, leaving the French throne for Napoleon's taking.

- **15/16 June 1815**
  The Armée du Nord invades Belgium and the battles of Quatre-Bras and Ligny are fought.

- **18 June 1815**

  - **07:00–08:00**
    Wellington inspects his army at Mont-Saint-Jean while Napoleon takes breakfast at Le Caillou. Meanwhile Bülow's IV Corps has left Wavre, heading for the Waterloo battlefield.

  - **08:30–09:30**
    Napoleon surveys the positions of Wellington's Anglo-Allied army from La Belle Alliance.

  - **09:30–10:00**
    The 1/2nd Nassau-Usingen Regiment is ordered to reinforce the light companies of the Guards in Hougoumont. Blücher despatches a note to Wellington stating he is marching to his position.

  - **10:00–11:00**
    Lieutenant-Colonel Macdonnell redeploys his Guards light companies to the west of the Hougoumont buildings and the kitchen garden, while the 1/2nd Nassau-Usingen Regiment takes up positions in the buildings and orchard.

  - **11:00–12:30**
    Napoleon outlines his orders for the coming attack before conducting a review of his army. The battle opens at approximately 11:30 and Jérôme's assault on Hougoumont begins. Baudin's 1st Brigade drives the Brunswick and Nassau troops from the orchard, but the orchard is subsequently retaken by the Guards.

  - **12:30–13:30**
    Jérôme commits Soye's 2nd Brigade to the assault on Hougoumont, and Cubiéres

is wounded by Sergeant Fraser. The Grande Batterie opens fire in preparation for d'Erlon's advance, while Napoleon spots Prussian troops in the distance.

13:30–14:30
D'Erlon begins his advance and elements of Quiot's division assault La Haye-Sainte. Four of Bijlandt's five demoralised mixed Dutch and Belgian battalions break, opening a 250-metre gap in Wellington's line. Sir Thomas Picton is killed while leading a counter-attack. Uxbridge orders his Household and Union brigades to charge.

14:30–15:00
D'Erlon's corps is driven back in disorder by the British heavy cavalry, but they are in turn counter-attacked by French *cuirassiers* and *lanciers*. Campi's 2nd Brigade marches to attack Hougoumont but is driven back by Anglo-Allied artillery fire.

15:00–16:00
Some of the buildings at Hougoumont are set alight by French artillery fire and Quiot renews his attack on La Haye-Sainte. Ney mistakes movements along Wellington's line as a withdrawal and orders his cavalry to attack.

16:00–17:00
Ney personally leads forward ten regiments of *cuirassiers*, *chasseurs* and *lanciers*, but Wellington has ordered his infantry into squares on the reverse slope. Ney's first cavalry attack fails but he orders repeated attacks. Lobau's VI Corps engages Bülow's IV Corps as the Prussians pour out of the Bois de Paris.

17:00–18:00
The French cavalry attacks continue but are unsuccessful, finally ending around 18:00. The 13e Léger begins its attack on La Haye-Sainte while the Prussians push Lobau's men back towards Plancenoit.

18:00–19:30
Plancenoit is taken by the Prussian 15th and 16th brigades, but they are driven out by Duhesme's Young Guard. The Prussians counter-attack and retake the village, but again are driven out by the Old Guard. La Haye-Sainte falls to the French. Zieten's I Corps arrives at Ohain.

19:30–20:30
Wellington redeploys his reserves to reinforce his battered centre. Napoleon orders the Middle and Old Guard to begin their attack; however, they are mauled by Wellington's artillery and infantry, including a flank attack by the 52nd Foot. Units from Pirch's Prussian II Corps launch a final assault on Plancenoit.

20:30–22:00
With the defeat of the Garde Impériale the French army begins to disintegrate and Wellington orders a general advance. Plancenoit is now in Prussian hands and they begin to march towards La Belle Alliance. Wellington and Blücher finally meet at La Belle Alliance and agree that the Prussians will carry out the pursuit of the French army.

22 June 1815
Napoleon abdicates for the second time and is eventually sent into exile on Saint Helena.

5 May 1821
Napoleon dies of suspected stomach cancer, although some believe he was poisoned.

Napoleon Bonaparte, who rose rapidly from relative obscurity to become emperor of the French. (Rijksmuseum)

1

THE RISE OF NAPOLEON

Napoleon Bonaparte was born in Ajaccio, Corsica, on 15 August 1769, being christened Napoleone di Buonaparte. During the year of his birth the island of Corsica was transferred from the Republic of Genoa to France, and in later life he would change to his more French-sounding name. His parents, Carlo and Maria Letizia, had a total of thirteen children, although only eight would survive beyond infancy. After his rise to power Napoleon would install certain members of his family in positions of authority, including his brothers Joseph (as King of Naples and Sicily and later Spain), Louis (as King of Holland) and Jérôme (as King of Westphalia.) However, the future emperor's family was, in a time when social standing meant everything, only of minor nobility. So how did Napoleon go from being a relative nobody to the most powerful man in Europe?

THE FRENCH REVOLUTION

It is perhaps the French Revolution of 1789–99 that provided Napoleon the opportunities to begin his ascent to power. Indeed, it would be the Revolution that led Europe to war in 1792, a conflict that would last virtually uninterrupted for almost a quarter of a century. Napoleon would use his military talents during these wars to come to the attention of leaders of the Revolution, and when the time was right he seized power over all of France.

The French Revolution itself was not a single event, rather a series of developments over the period of more than a decade. It resulted in a feeling of uncertainty, bloody disorder and conflict, which would spill beyond the borders of France. Prior to 1789 there had been a growing resentment among ordinary French people towards the seemingly privileged lives enjoyed by the aristocracy and the powerful clergy. Along with this resentment was the ongoing financial crisis that France was experiencing in the late eighteenth century, a crisis that had been triggered by King Louis XVI.

Louis XVI, the unpopular King of France who would be deposed and later executed during the French Revolution. (Rijksmuseum)

France had fought a number of wars against Britain, her long-standing rival, including the more recent Seven Years' War (1756–63) and the American War of Independence (1775–83). These wars had created massive debts for France, but Louis XVI had hoped supporting the Americans in their bid for independence would result in increased trade with the emergent United States. Although the defeat of the British in North America owed much to French help, the newly independent US continued its trade with Britain, leaving France with greater war debts and none of the hoped-for lucrative trading rights.

At this time France was an absolute monarchy, known as the *Ancien Régime* (Old Order), and the king's decision was final. This authority was exercised over the country through the Intendants, of which there was one for each of the thirty-six *généralités* into which France was divided. All of the Intendants were appointed from the ranks of the nobility, but their strict authoritarian ways made them unpopular with the people.

To further exacerbate these issues a hailstorm in 1789 destroyed much of the harvests of northern France, and there was little in the way of reserves. The price of bread rose sharply and the French people were forced to spend most of their meagre income on feeding themselves. Manufacturers also found competition with the British, who were undercutting their French competitors, increasingly difficult, and large numbers of workers inevitably lost their jobs.

In an attempt to address the political unrest, Les États Généraux (the Estates General), which represented the clergy (First Estate), the nobility (Second Estate) and everybody else (Third Estate), was convened. This was the first time it had met since 1614, and the delegates representing all three estates were told to produce a *cahiers de doléances* (list of grievances) for a meeting on 5 May. The Third Estate by far made up the majority of the delegates, yet under the voting system they could still be out-voted by the other two. Perhaps unsurprisingly, members of the Third Estate demanded this imbalance be addressed, but the other two estates were unwilling to give up their political privileges. The 5 May meeting took place at the Grands Salles des Menus-Plaisirs in Versailles, but following a boring three-hour speech by Jacques Necker, the French finance minister, in-fighting between the estates resulted in the original purpose of the meeting being lost.

Emmanuel Joseph Sieyès, a Catholic clergymen (known as Abbé Sieyès) and supporter of the Third Estate, suggested the Third Estate meet on its own in June. At the meeting they voted to declare themselves the National Assembly, a body that was to do the business of France with or without the other estates. On 20 June they again met at an indoor tennis court, where they took the so-called Serment du Jeu de Paume (Tennis Court Oath), swearing not to cease their activities until constitutional reform was achieved. Later, members of the other two estates joined the National Assembly, and although Louis XVI initially attempted to stop it, he eventually agreed to its creation. This change of stance was likely due to the high level of support the National Assembly was attracting both in Paris and elsewhere across France.

On 11 July, Necker publically published information about the government's accounts, and a furious Louis XVI sacked him. This was seen by the French people as a move against the National Assembly, and to make matters worse the king ordered up troops to Versailles. Soon some 20,000 soldiers were encamped around the Île-de-France and, despite the king's assurances that their presence was merely to maintain public order, many believed the army was about to overthrow the National Assembly. Rioting ensued, and a mob stormed the Bastille prison on 14 July. After several hours the prison was taken and its governor, the Marquis Bernard de Launay, met a grisly end.

On 4 August the National Assembly adopted the 'Déclaration des droits de l'homme et du citoyen' (Declaration of the Rights of Man and Citizen), a

The storming of the medieval fortress Bastille on 14 July 1789 was perhaps the flashpoint of the French Revolution. (The British Library Board)

document that promised to replace the *Ancien Régime* with a system of equality and freedom of speech. The National Assembly, however, inherited all the economic and social problems suffered under the previous system of government. Initially Louis XVI was allowed to remain king, albeit with much reduced authority, but on 13 August 1792 he was arrested and France was declared a Republic on 21 September. The former king was put on trial and, after being found guilty of 'colluding with invaders', he was executed by guillotine at the Place de la Révolution on 21 January 1793.

Later in June the Jacobins would seize control of the National Convention (a successor to the National Assembly), and the Revolution would take on a more sinister form. The calendar was abolished, as part of the Jacobins' drive to eradicate religion, and replaced with the *Calendrier Républicain Français* (French Republican Calendar). They also later imposed *La Terreur* (The Terror), the mass executions of 'enemies of the revolution', which was eagerly prosecuted by the most influential Jacobin of all, Maximilien de Robespierre. As the killings, particularly of the aristocracy, increased, the other European powers looked on in horror.

THE FRENCH REVOLUTIONARY WARS

One way in which the Revolution coped with internal struggle was war, and they were not short of enemies abroad. War, they reasoned, would help unite the nation against an external threat, drawing attention away from domestic issues. With that, the survival of the Revolution became one and the same as the survival of the nation.

What we today call the French Revolutionary Wars were in fact two separate conflicts, known as the War of the First Coalition (1792–97) and the War of the Second Coalition (1798–1802). These conflicts are important because they forced political, social and military changes on a massive scale that would reshape the Western world forever. The wars also made the peoples of Europe question the principle of monarchy, a political system that had long underpinned much of the continent. When the French people removed the *Ancien Régime* they began to lay the foundations of democratic and constitutional rule, and where the French armies went these principles followed. Fighting took place across the globe, including western and central Europe, the Middle East, southern Africa and the West Indies. The battles would be fought by mass citizen armies, with many of the protagonist nations mobilising resources on a scale not previously seen.

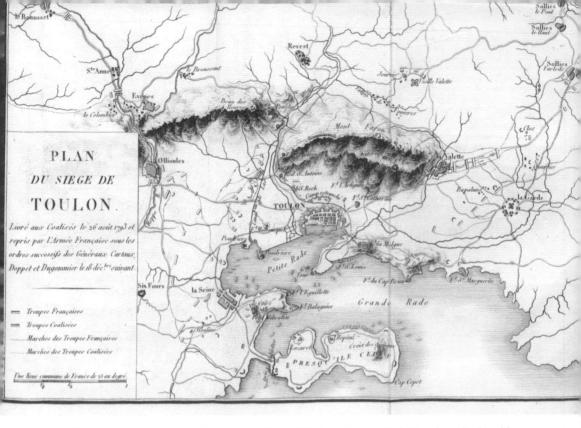

French revolutionary period map of the Siege of Toulon, during which Napoleon displayed his remarkable military talents. (The British Library Board)

It would be during mid-1793 that Napoleon, as a junior artillery officer in the French revolutionary army, came to the attention of Augustin de Robespierre, the younger brother of Maximilien de Robespierre, when he published a pro-revolutionary political pamphlet called 'Le souper de Beaucaire' (Supper at Beaucaire). Augustin liked what he read and, when the port city of Toulon in the south of France rose in open revolt against the Revolution, Napoleon found himself in command of revolutionary forces sent to subdue the city.

The royalists in the city looked to the British for help, the latter responding by sending a fleet of ships, under command of Admiral Sir Samuel Hood, as well as landing a number of troops. If having foreign troops on French soil was not bad enough, about a third of the French navy's ships were trapped in the port. This was a major blow to the prestige of not only France but the Revolution itself. However, Napoleon formulated a striking plan to use artillery on positions overlooking Toulon's harbour, which he hoped would persuade the British to withdraw their precious ships. Eventually the British did abandon Toulon, and Napoleon, at the age of only twenty-four, was promoted to brigadier in the French Armée d'Italie (Army of Italy).

In October 1795, royalists again rose in rebellion in Paris. Aware of Napoleon's success at Toulon, Paul Barras, a prominent figure in the Thermidorian Reaction that had overthrown Maximilien de Robespierre the previous year, placed him in command of the troops in the capital. As an artillery officer, Napoleon made use of cannon to put an end to the rebellion when on 5 October (known as vendémiaire an IV in the French Republican Calendar) he deployed artillery to repel a royalist attack. The battle lasted for several hours, during which Napoleon ordered canister shot to be used, resulting in many deaths among the royalist ranks and forcing the remainder to flee. This 'whiff of grapeshot', as it would later be termed by historian Thomas Carlyle (grapeshot is actually the naval version of canister shot), catapulted Napoleon to fame throughout France. It would also give him the support of the Directory, which had replaced the National Convention in November. Perhaps more importantly, he was promoted to overall command of the Armée d'Italie.

Napoleon would go on to conduct two major campaigns during the French Revolutionary Wars, including his Italian campaign (1796–97) and his expedition to Egypt (1798–1801). The former was by far more successful than the latter, leading to the Treaty of Campo Formio, which saw the collapse of the First Coalition, as well as the ceding of Belgium to France with the Rhineland and large sections of Italy falling under French control. The Egyptian campaign, aimed at seizing Egypt in the hope of harming British trade with India, saw initial success against the Mamluks, but British intervention led to Napoleon's army being cut off and trapped. Before the campaign ended Napoleon passed command of his army to Jean Baptiste Kléber on 24 August 1799 and left for France, leaving his disgruntled soldiers to fight on until late 1801.

Back in France, Napoleon was treated as a hero, and he decided the time was right to make his bid for power over the country, entering into an alliance with director Abbé Sieyès, minister of police Joseph Fouché, foreign minister Charles Maurice de Talleyrand-Périgord, and his brother Lucien in an attempt to overthrow the Directory. The bid was successful when, on 9 November 1799 (18th Brumaire), in a *coup d'état*, he shut down the Council of Five Hundred (the lower house of the Directory). Napoleon became first consul, which was written into a new constitution. Although in theory France was still a republic it had in fact become a dictatorship, which would be confirmed on 2 December 1804 when Napoleon was crowned emperor.

THE NAPOLEONIC WARS

The French Revolutionary Wars eventually ended in 1802, but by the following year Napoleon would again be at war with Britain. Between 1803 and 1815 a series of wars would be fought, including the War of the Third Coalition (1805), War of the Fourth Coalition (1806–07), War of the Fifth Coalition (1809), War of the Sixth Coalition (1812–14) and War of the Seventh Coalition (1815). It would be during the latter that the Battle of Waterloo, as part of the Hundred Days, took place. In addition there were a number of other conflicts, including the Peninsular War (1807–14), the War of 1812 against America (1812–15) and Napoleon's disastrous invasion of Russia (1812).

France had already seen victory in both the Wars of the First and Second Coalitions, and the subsequent conflicts provided Napoleon with yet more victories. Perhaps Napoleon's most notable battles were those of Austerlitz (5 December 1805), Jena–Auerstädt (14 October 1806), Eylau (7–8 February 1807), Friedland (14 June 1807) and Wagram (5–6 July 1809). Indeed, it is claimed that of the sixty battles Napoleon fought he only lost seven.

Things began to go wrong for Napoleon from 1812, when he mounted his ill-fated invasion of Russia. As with his earlier Egyptian campaign, the fighting initially went well for the emperor, achieving victory at the Battle of Borodino (7 September 1812), although he failed to destroy the Russian army. He then went on to capture Moscow, but a fire had broken out which engulfed much of the city. With winter fast approaching, Napoleon eventually decided to withdraw, and along the march back to France he lost most of his army in what would be a horrendous journey in bitter conditions while being harassed by Russian forces.

By 1814 defeat seemed inevitable for Napoleon, with the forces of the Sixth Coalition (including Austria, Prussia, Russia, Britain, Portugal, Sweden, Spain and a number of small German states) slowly closing in on France from multiple directions. At the Battle of Leipzig (16–19 October 1813) Napoleon had suffered a massive defeat at the hands of a combined Russian, Prussian, Austrian and

Opposite top: The Battle of the Pyramids, 21 July 1798, where Napoleon inflicted a crushing defeat on the Mamluks during his Egyptian campaign. (Anne S. K. Brown Military Collection, Brown University Library)

Opposite bottom: At the Battle of Wagram, Napoleon fought a decisive action against the Austrians on 5/6 July 1809 during the War of the Fifth Coalition. (Anne S. K. Brown Military Collection, Brown University Library)

Swedish force under Alexander I, the Emperor of Russia. With the situation fast deteriorating, Napoleon was confronted on 4 April 1814 by his own *maréchals* and *généraux*, who refused to continue what was now a hopeless fight. At first Napoleon refused to give in, but on 6 April he finally abdicated, and the War of the Sixth Coalition was over.

The victorious powers now had to deal with a defeated Napoleon, who still seemed to pose a threat to the stability of Europe. It was, therefore, decided to send him into exile, where he could live out his life away from European affairs. The place of exile was to be the island of Elba off the Tuscan coast, where he would be allowed to rule as sovereign and retain his title emperor. However, it would not be the last Europe would see of Napoleon Bonaparte.

A typical Georgian period political cartoon depicting Napoleon's exile to Elba.

2

PRELUDE TO WATERLOO

On 20 April 1814 Napoleon addressed the men of his beloved Old Guard to bid them farewell. He then set off for Fréjus in south-eastern France, where he boarded the waiting British frigate HMS *Undaunted* for the crossing to Elba and to begin a new life in exile.

EXILE AND ESCAPE FROM ELBA

The emperor arrived in Elba on 3 May, where the 12,000 inhabitants had only been informed about their new ruler the day before. Napoleon would take up residence at I Mulini, an eighteenth-century house built by the Medicis for the gardener of a former governor. Initially he enjoyed playing ruler, reorganising the administration of the island and ordering the construction of a new theatre. He also had plans to reform Elba's agriculture, which principally included the growing of olives, mulberries, chestnuts and potatoes.

Few of Napoleon's schemes came to fruition, mainly due to lack of funds. Under the terms of the Treaty of Fontainebleau (an agreement between Napoleon and the members of the Sixth Coalition), the newly installed French king, Louis XVIII, who was brother of the executed Louis XVI, was to pay Napoleon 2 million francs per annum. With the emperor now out of the way the payments never materialised, and Napoleon's enthusiasm quickly dissipated. To make matters worse he found himself with little to occupy his time, spending his days feeling dispirited and reflecting on what had gone wrong during his reign.

The 4 million francs Napoleon had been allowed to take with him to Elba were quickly spent and he was unable to pay members of his Old Guard and Polish Lancers, who had joined him in exile as bodyguards. This led to increased fears of assassination, and the British worried that Napoleon might attempt escape. Lord Castlereagh, the British Secretary of State for Foreign Affairs, raised the issue of non-payment with Louis XVIII, but no direct reply was received. Escape was

LOUIS XVIII *le désiré*.
Roi de France et de Navarre,
Né à Versailles, le 17. Nov. 1755.

Louis XVIII, brother of the executed Louis XVI, who was installed on the throne of France following the emperor's first abdication. He would be forced to flee to Ghent on the night of 19/20 March 1815, leaving the throne for Napoleon's taking. (Anne S. K. Brown Military Collection, Brown University Library)

indeed on the emperor's mind, and furthermore he planned to retake the throne of France.

On 16 February 1815, Colonel Sir Neil Campbell, the British commissioner on Elba charged with keeping an eye on Napoleon, left the island for a medical consultation in Florence. Campbell made his journey aboard HMS *Partridge*, the Royal Navy warship patrolling the seas around the island. Napoleon grasped this opportunity and gave orders for the brig *Inconstant* to be fitted out for the voyage to France. Another six smaller craft were also utilised to carry arms, ammunition and men, the latter of which would include 650 of his Old Guard, just over 100 Polish Lancers and a number of volunteers from Corsica and Elba.

The voyage was uneventful and an encounter with the French warship *Zéphyr* failed to detect *Inconstant*'s special passenger. On 28 February Napoleon and his army, numbering 1,026 men, forty horses and two cannon, landed at Golfe-Juan near Antibes. This tiny army then embarked on the long march to Paris, during which it would encounter a force of the 5e Régiment de Ligne near Laffrey. As the two forces confronted each other the emperor rode ahead before dismounting. Walking to within musket range, he paused before saying, 'Soldiers of the 5e Ligne, if there is a soldier among you who wishes to kill his emperor, he may do so.' The men sent to oppose Napoleon replied with shouts of '*Vive l'Empereur!*'

Increasing numbers of French troops would join the emperor, including Michel Ney, one of Napoleon's former *maréchals*. Ney, following news of the emperor's advance on Paris, was recalled by the king to oppose him, and it would be Ney who allegedly boasted that he would bring Bonaparte back to Paris in an iron cage. As the emperor advanced on Paris, Louis XVIII fled France for Ghent on the night of 19/20 March, leaving the throne for the taking. Napoleon's bid for power had succeeded once again.

THE OPPOSING STRATEGIES

Napoleon knew the Allied powers would not accept him as the legitimate ruler of France and that war would likely follow. On 13 March the Congress of Vienna labelled him an outlaw and declared war on him personally. It is important to understand that France was not the enemy, the emperor was. Indeed, France would be invited to take its place at the congress following Napoleon's final defeat in June 1815.

The basic strategy of the Allies was to send an overwhelming force of 700,000 men into France under the command of the Austrian Feldmarschall Karl Philipp, Fürst zu Schwarzenberg. The purpose being to remove the emperor, while Castlereagh also secretly wanted to restore Louis XVIII to the French throne. The armies included those of Austria, Russia, Prussia and an Anglo-Allied force. However, both Austria and Russia would take several months to assemble their armies, leaving the Prussian army and Anglo-Allies, already in the Low Counties, waiting in Belgium.

Meanwhile Napoleon had set about raising 40 million francs and placed orders for the manufacture of 250,000 stands of arms, while the French Ministry of War pledged that 46,000 horses would be ready by 1 June. He dreamed of raising an army of 800,000, which he calculated could be ready by early October. However, he knew the Allied powers would most likely make their move long before then. Realistically Napoleon had two options open to him: stay on the defensive and wait for his additional troops, or go on the offensive in the Low Countries and deal a pre-emptive knock-out blow against the Prussian and Anglo-Allied armies.

The Congress of Vienna was convened following Napoleon's abdication in 1814, its aim to ensure a lasting peace in Europe. After Napoleon's escape from Elba, the congress declared war on him personally. (Anne S. K. Brown Military Collection, Brown University Library)

It would be the offensive that Napoleon pinned his hopes on for victory, but the army maintained by the Bourbon king numbered less than 200,000 men. He did, however, manage to raise a number of additional troops, which included discharged veterans, National Guardsmen, policemen, customs officials, sailors and others. However, many would be 'ineffectives', and the actual number available for operations would still be relatively low. Not all his troops would be available as a single army either, since the likely routes the Allies might take to Paris would need to be defended. There was also an outbreak of royalist unrest in the Vendée during mid-May, which forced the diversion of valuable troops to restore order.

The emperor planned to invade Belgium and position his force between the Prussian and Anglo-Allied armies (known as the strategy of the central position), after which he would defeat each in turn. This manoeuver was vital, otherwise the two armies combined would outnumber Napoleon's. The emperor was also aware that the British and Prussians held very different political views, and if he could drive a wedge between them the coalition might even collapse. However, some historians are now of the opinion that the emperor did not expect the

Allies in Belgium to stand and fight, rather they would retire along their lines of communication while he made his thrust towards Brussels.

THE OPPOSING ARMIES

Napoleon's Armée du Nord (Army of the North) began the Hundred Days campaign with approximately 123,000 men and 350 guns, although following the casualties sustained at the battles of Quatre-Bras and Ligny, this number would be reduced. Approximately another 30,000 men and ninety-six guns would also be detached to pursue the Prussians to Wavre, reducing it further still. As such it is estimated that the emperor had an approximate total of 77,500 men of all arms and 246 guns at Waterloo. The army was organised into five infantry corps, four cavalry corps and the Garde Impériale (Imperial Guard). These included: I Corps under d'Erlon; II Corps under Reille; III Corps under Vandamme; IV Corps under Gérard; VI Corps under Lobau; I Cavalry Corps under Pajol; II Cavalry Corps under Exelmans; III Cavalry Corps under Kellerman; IV Cavalry Corps under Milhaud; and the Garde Impériale under Drouot.

The Anglo-Allied army was commanded by Sir Arthur Wellesley, the Duke of Wellington, and, despite popular myth, much of it was not British. Only around a third of the army was made up of British regiments, and of those, few were veterans of the earlier wars. Other nationalities included Nassau, Brunswick, Hanoverian, Dutch and Belgian, as well as the men of the King's German Legion, all of whom played a part in the emperor's defeat. There was distrust of the Dutch and Belgians since many had previously fought under Napoleon and, coupled with the inexperience of the army overall, Wellington felt the need to intersperse his men. The duke's force totalled nearly 112,000 men and 204 guns, but after deducting the casualties at Quatre-Bras, the various garrisons he had to leave behind in Brussels and the force at Hal, the number available at Waterloo was around 73,200 supported by 157 guns. Of these, 36 per cent were British, while around 45 per cent spoke German. Wellington's army was organised into two infantry corps, including I Corps under the Prince of Orange-Nassau and II Corps under Lord Hill, a single cavalry corps under Uxbridge and a reserve, which he commanded himself.

Although not present at the beginning of the Battle of Waterloo, the Prussian army would play a crucial role in the defeat of Napoleon. This army was commanded by Feldmarschall Gebhard Leberecht von Blücher, who initially had a force of 130,000 men and 304 guns. Again, after subtracting the casualties at

Ligny and those who deserted or otherwise disappeared during the withdrawal to Wavre, this number was reduced to around 100,000 by 18 June. However, only 49,000 men and 134 guns would actually become engaged at Waterloo. Blücher's army was divided into four mixed corps, including: I Corps under Zieten, II Corps under Pirch, III Corps under Thielmann and IV Corps under Bülow.

THE ALLIED COMMANDERS

Sir Arthur Wellesley, 1st Duke of Wellington

Born on 1 May 1769 in Ireland, the son of Garret Wesley, 1st Earl of Mornington, and his wife, Anne. Despite being of Anglo-Irish aristocracy and educated at Eton, his early life was somewhat unremarkable. However, he later attended the Royal Academy of Equitation in Angers, and after showing improvement joined the army as an ensign in the 73rd Regiment of Foot in 1787. By 1793 he was the lieutenant-colonel of the 33rd Foot and saw active service under the Duke of York in Flanders before being posted to India. While in India, where his brother was Governor-General, Wellesley's military talents came to the fore, and between 1809 and 1814 he commanded a series of very successful actions against the French in Portugal and Spain during the Peninsular War. It was during his time on the Iberian Peninsula that he was promoted to field marshal and acquired the title the Duke of Wellington.

Gebhard Lebrecht, Fürst Blücher von Wahlstadt

Born on 16 December 1742 in Rostock in the Duchy of Mecklenberg-Schwerin, his father was a retired cavalry officer. He followed in his father's footsteps by joining a regiment of Hussars in the Swedish army aged fifteen. He would see active service during the Seven Years' War and later joined the Prussian army, becoming a generalmajor in 1794. It was with the Prussian army that he saw further active service throughout much of the Napoleonic Wars. However, it was when he was defeated at the Battle of Jena-Auerstädt in 1806 that he developed a bitter hatred of the French, although he would experience some feeling of revenge at the Battle of Leipzig, where Napoleon was defeated by the Sixth Coalition in 1813. At the time of the Battle of Waterloo he was seventy-two years old.

Sir Arthur Wellesley, 1st Duke of Wellington, who rose to become Britain's leading soldier following his successful campaigns in India and on the Iberian Peninsula. Despite his considerable active service, Waterloo was the first time he met Napoleon in battle. (Anne S. K. Brown Military Collection, Brown University Library)

QUATRE-BRAS AND LIGNY

The Battle of Waterloo was the third of four principal actions fought in Belgium during the Hundred Days campaign, and there were other minor skirmishes. The two that preceded it were Quatre-Bras and Ligny, both fought simultaneously on 16 June. Although any in-depth analysis of these actions is beyond the scope of this book, it is perhaps useful to briefly consider some key points. The fourth, the Battle of Wavre, is also briefly examined in the final chapter.

At 02:30 on 15 June 1815, the emperor's army crossed the border into Belgium at Leers-et-Fosteau, Cour-sur-Heure and Thy-le-Château. At 03:30, French troops clashed with Prussian outposts in and around the village of Thuin near Charleroi. By 18:00 Wellington had given orders for his army to begin concentrating, but he was unsure where Napoleon's main thrust would come. However, by about midnight he was convinced that it was indeed Charleroi and gave further orders for his army to move towards Quatre-Bras.

Quatre-Bras, meaning 'crossroads', was strategically important since it commanded the Nivelles–Namur road. If the French could hold Quatre-Bras it would prevent Wellington marching to assist Blücher, whom the emperor now planned to attack first. Napoleon ordered Ney to take the French I Corps under Général de Division Jean-Baptiste Drouet (Comte d'Erlon), II Corps under the command of Général de Division Honoré Charles Reille and the III Cavalry Corps under Général de Division François Étienne de Kellermann, to seize the crossroads. The emperor would then engage Blücher's army and, if possible, once Ney had dealt with Wellington he was to come to the aid of Napoleon by mounting an attack of the Prussian rear.

It would not be until late the following morning that Ney's troops advanced on Quatre-Bras. By this time, units of Wellington's army under Willem Frederik George Lodewijk van Oranje-Nassau (Prince of Orange-Nassau) had already begun arriving and the battle commenced. Throughout the action the French were unable to dislodge the Allies, and although Ney prevented Wellington coming to the aid of Blücher, his failure to seize Quatre-Bras and come to the assistance of his emperor would have serious consequences.

At this point it should also be noted that d'Erlon's I Corps spent much of the day marching back and forth between Quatre-Bras and Ligny, responding to conflicting orders issued by Ney and Napoleon. As such it took no part in either action which, it has been argued, had a detrimental result on the emperor's whole 1815 campaign.

Maréchal Michel Ney, known affectionately as '*le Rougeaud*' by his men and described as '*le Brave des Braves*' by Napoleon on account of his bravery in battle. At Waterloo he would personally lead repeated attacks against the Anglo-Allied line and have five horses shot from under him. (Courtesy of Andrew Field)

Willem Frederik George Lodewijk van Oranje-Nassau, who commanded I Corps of the Anglo-Allied army. Although later heavily criticised by historians, the prince was courageous in battle, being wounded at Waterloo leading a counter-attack against the Garde Impériale. (Anne S. K. Brown Military Collection, Brown University Library)

The 7th Queen's Own Hussars, a British light cavalry regiment, engaging French infantry at Quatre-Bras. (Anne S. K. Brown Military Collection, Brown University Library)

Meanwhile, Napoleon had engaged Blücher's army at St Amand and Ligny. He had heard the sound of gunfire from Quatre-Bras and, knowing Ney had begun his action, he began his own attack. The battle would see much bitter fighting, and at one point the village of Ligny itself was set alight by artillery fire. Eventually the emperor's Old Guard managed to break the centre of Blücher's line, forcing the Prussians to withdraw. Although defeated, the Prussian army was not destroyed and would survive largely intact to fight at Waterloo.

THE DAY AND NIGHT BEFORE

Following the Prussian defeat at Ligny, Wellington had little choice but to abandon Quatre-Bras on 17 June, withdrawing his army northwards. The duke decided to head for Mont-Saint-Jean, south of a village called Waterloo. It was not by accident that he chose this location, since he knew the ground and believed it to be a good defensive position. The Prussians conducted their own withdrawal, and crucially Blücher had also decided to go north towards the Belgian town of Wavre. This allowed him to keep on a parallel course and stay in contact with Wellington. The feldmarschall, despite protestations from some of his senior officers who distrusted the British commander, was determined to keep his word to come to the aid of the duke.

After some delay, Napoleon marched his army to Quatre-Bras, where he was rejoined by Ney. The emperor had hoped to engage Wellington at the crossroads, but by the time he arrived the duke and his men had gone. A pursuit began and elements of both armies fought a brief skirmish at Genappe, but heavy rain and fading daylight meant there would be no prospect of a major battle that day.

Before leaving Ligny, Napoleon had instructed Maréchal Emmanuel de Grouchy to take 30,000 men and ninety-six cannon to pursue the Prussians in order to prevent them moving to support Wellington. However, Grouchy was slow off the mark, being unsure where the Prussians were heading, and failed to harass the retreating army. In fact the Prussians were able to reach Wavre with little interference, and they began to regroup here.

Wellington's army was by now arriving at Mont-Saint-Jean, but his men would have to endure a night under torrential rain. Few had the benefit of shelter and most would begin the following day soaked to the skin and caked in mud. The duke, however, had the relative comforts of the coaching inn at Waterloo, where after a brief spell in bed he would rise at 03:00 to begin writing his many letters that night. It is said that the tone of these letters betrayed the duke's concern about meeting the emperor in battle the next day. However, he had by now received word from Blücher stating that he was moving to support him.

The emperor also enjoyed shelter from the elements, having taken up temporary residence at the farm of Le Caillou, where one of his servants had set up his camp bed and lit a fire. Napoleon later claimed to have left the farmhouse that night and made his way on foot to where his army had bivouacked, after which he walked the French line. However, some historians believe this claim to be untrue, since no one but the emperor has ever mentioned the fact.

HAL AND TUBIZE

Wellington held concerns that the French might attempt a thrust along the Mons–Hal–Brussels route towards the Belgian capital. To guard against this potential threat he detached two of three brigades from Lieutenant-General Sir Charles Colville's 4th British Infantry Division (part of Lieutenant-General Lord Rowland Hill's II Corps) to the villages of Hal and Tubize. He also deployed to the villages Lieutenant-General John Stedman's 1st Netherlands Infantry Division, bringing the combined total to around 17,000 men. The force at Hal and Tubize played no part in the Battle of Waterloo, despite being only two or three hours' march away, and the duke later received criticism for his decision to detach this significant portion of his army.

Lieutenant-General Lord Rowland Hill, who commanded II Corps of the Anglo-Allied army. Hill served alongside Wellington throughout the Peninsular War, and at Waterloo he led Adam's 3rd Brigade forward against the Garde Impériale. (Anne S. K. Brown Military Collection, Brown University Library)

3

PHASE 1: HOUGOUMONT

The Battle of Waterloo was not actually fought at Waterloo, the village being five kilometres to the north of the battle site. At the time, and indeed in the years since, many have argued the battle should have been given a more appropriate name. These include the Battle of Mont-Saint-Jean, the Battle of Plancenoit and the Battle of Belle Alliance – all named after components of the battlefield. However, after the battle Wellington would go back to the inn at Waterloo, from where he wrote his famous despatch. As such the British quickly began to refer to it as the 'Battle of Waterloo', a name which stuck, albeit to the dismay of many non-British protagonists.

THE BATTLEFIELD

The area around Mont-Saint-Jean was predominately farmland which was bisected from north to south by the Brussels–Genappe–Charleroi road. This road was joined by another leading from Nivelles, and holding the position meant blocking two of three possible routes the emperor might take to Brussels. The location was also less than twelve kilometres from Wavre, where Blücher was regrouping, and to the rear was the Forest of Soignes, which stretched for approximately eight to ten kilometres, after which were the southern approaches to Brussels. As such, the position of Mont-Saint-Jean was strategically important.

As with most battlefields, there were a number of key features of importance. The first was the ridge of Mont-Saint-Jean, which, although low, ran south-west to north-east approximately 700 metres to the south of the Mont-Saint-Jean farmhouse. Along this crest ran the Braine l'Alleud–Ohain road (dissecting the Brussels–Genappe–Charleroi road), which would form the front line of Wellington's army along an approximate 1,500–metre front. Opposite was the Belle Alliance ridge, which ran south-west from the south of the village of

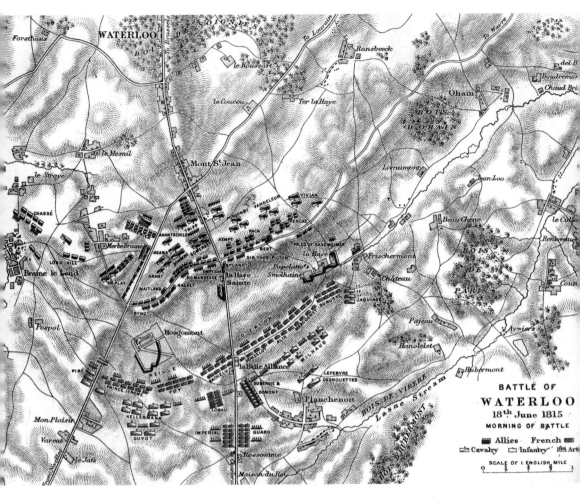

Battle of Waterloo map showing deployment of the armies on the morning of 18 June 1815.

Papelotte, through the Belle Alliance, then north-west towards Braine l'Alleud curving around Hougoumont. This ridge, which ranged from 350 to 1,400 metres from the duke's front line, formed the line along which Napoleon would deploy his army.

Two buildings that would be focal points during the fighting were the château and farmhouses of Hougoumont and La Haye-Sainte. The former was 400 metres forward of Wellington's right flank, and if properly defended would help protect his right. The latter was also forward of the line (by 250 metres), this time to the centre of the duke's position on the western side of the Brussels–Genappe–Charleroi road. In addition there was a sandpit on the opposite side of the road about fifty metres north of La Haye-Sainte. Again, if properly defended, these positions would pose a serious obstacle to any assault up the main road.

Other key features of the battlefield included the Papelotte, La Haye, Smohain and Fichermont farms and villages over on Wellington's left flank, and the so-called 'Grand Battery' ridge located roughly halfway between La Haye-Sainte and La Belle Alliance. Finally, there was also the farming community of Plancenoit located behind the emperor's front line to his right. This village would be a critical site of much bitter fighting between French and Prussian troops during the latter phases of the battle.

Generally speaking, infantry would be deployed along the opposing lines, while the cavalry tended to be held slightly further back or on the flanks. Artillery would also be placed along the front, ready to open up a bombardment. On both sides men would be seen cleaning their weapons, feeding and watering their horses, and those lucky enough to have food ate it. Many of Wellington's men would also be given a ration of gin, while those of Napoleon's army drank brandy, at least the fortunate few to receive it.

La Haye-Sainte after the Battle of Waterloo. Garrisoned by men of the King's German Legion, the farm fell to the French only after a staunch defence conducted by Major Georg Baring. (The British Library Board)

Jérôme Bonaparte, brother of Napoleon and commanding officer of the 6th French Infantry Division. Due to his inexperience he was assisted by Général de Division Armand Guilleminot. (Courtesy of Andrew Field)

As Wellington supervised the deployment of his troops, Napoleon ate breakfast at Le Caillou. He was urged by some of his senior officers to recall Grouchy, but the emperor furiously dismissed the suggestion, arguing that the Prussians had been beaten at Ligny and would need time to recover. However, Napoleon would be forced to delay the beginning of the battle due to the weather, the rain-soaked ground having impeded his army's preparations.

At 11:00 the emperor dictated orders for the coming battle to Maréchal Nicolas Jean-de-Dieu Soult, his chief of staff. The heavy twelve-pounder guns of I, II and VI Corps were to commence a bombardment of the Anglo-Allied centre at 13:00, after which d'Erlon's I Corps was expected to advance on the village of Mont-Saint-Jean with Reille's II Corps in support. The attack would be coordinated by Ney while Général de Division Georges Mouton, Comte de Lobau's VI Corps, the Garde Impériale and the cavalry were to remain in reserve. Later the emperor would also direct Prince Jérôme Bonaparte's 6th and

Maximilien Sebastien Foy's 9th infantry divisions (both from II Corps) to mount a diversionary assault on Hougoumont and its environs. The latter, Napoleon hoped, would force Wellington to divert some of his reserves for its defence.

THE BATTLE BEGINS: THE STRUGGLE FOR HOUGOUMONT

There is some dispute as to the actual time the battle began, Wellington recording it in his despatch at about 10:00 while others believe it to have been around 11:30. The British had their watches set to GMT and so were one hour behind their French counterparts, which may help explain some of the discrepancy. However, many historians believe it to be around 11:30 when, despite Napoleon's original orders, Reille's II Corps began its advance about an hour earlier than planned. At the same time the sound of cannon fire rang out across the battlefield, signalling the Battle of Waterloo was underway.

HOUGOUMONT

Hougoumont consisted of a number of buildings, including a château, a chapel, the farmer's house, stables, the great barn and store sheds. There were also northern and southern courtyards linked via an archway with a door. The complex was accessed by a number of gates, including one to the north and one to the south, as well as a door that led to a kitchen garden. Outside the complex was a formal garden to the east, which was partly surrounded by a wall, a kitchen garden to the west, a wood to the south and an orchard to the east and north. Also to the north was the sunken way, a track with a thick hedge on its southern side.

Before the battle Wellington had garrisoned Hougoumont with two light companies from the British 2nd Coldstream Guards and 2/3rd Foot Guards, the 1/2nd Nassau-Usingen Regiment under Captain Moritz Büsgen and 200 Brunswick troops – totaling 1,210 men. These troops had fortified the position, including digging loopholes in walls through which to fire their muskets. Overall command was given to Lieutenant-Colonel James Macdonnell of the Coldstream Guards, and throughout the battle the duke would order more and more men into the defence under increasing pressure from French attacks.

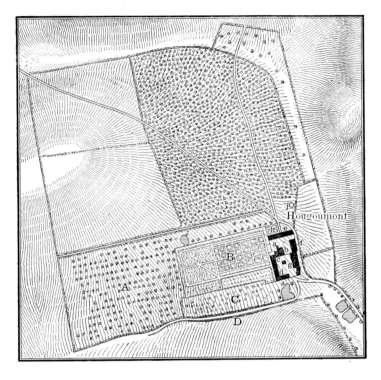

Plan of
Hougoumont.
(The British
Library Board)

However, it would be Jérôme's assault upon Hougoumont that would form
the first major phase of the battle. Although nominally placing him in command,
Napoleon felt his brother to be inexperienced and so he was assisted by Général
de Division Armand Guilleminot. The initial assault was made at 11:30 by the 1er
Régiment d'Infanterie Légère of Maréchal de Camp Pierre Bauduin's 1st Brigade
following an artillery bombardment. As the *tirailleurs* (skirmishers) advanced
towards the elm wood to the south of Hougoumont, the British artillery situated
on the ridge above the château opened a devastating fire on the French infantry
columns. Despite this, Jérôme's men continued to advance and came into contact
with Brunswick *jaegars* (riflemen) and Nassau skirmishers. During this fight in
the wood Bauduin would be shot dead and command of the brigade would pass
to Colonel Amédée Despans-Cubières.

Despite the loss of Bauduin and the deadly fire from the Brunswick riflemen,
the French *tirailleurs* kept up their pressure and after a few minutes, through
sheer weight of numbers, began to push back the *jaegars*, who were running low
on ammunition. Their Nassau counterparts also began to fall back, some making
it to the château to continue the defence while others headed back to the main
Anglo-Allied line. The *tirailleurs* now reached the garden wall and the rear of the

Hougoumont buildings, but as they pushed forward and entered open ground from the wood they came under intense fire from the Nassau defenders. The Guards then began to drive the French infantrymen back into the wood, but as the British troops reached the wood themselves the French opened a heavy fire on the Guardsmen.

Anxious about the defence of Hougoumont, Wellington had been watching the action from high ground overlooking the complex and ordered six howitzers, under Major Robert Bull of the Royal Horse Artillery, to come forward. Unlike normal artillery, howitzers literally lob their shot from a high angle, thus being able to hit targets other artillery could not. As such, they began to explode shrapnel shells above the French infantrymen in the wood, causing significant casualties and forcing them to withdraw. By 12:15 the Guards had recaptured the wood.

Seeing that the gains made by his men had been lost, Jérôme ordered the two battalions of the 3e Régiment de Ligne from his 2nd Brigade, under Maréchal de Camp Jean-Louis Soye, to advance in support of his struggling 1st Brigade. As

Although wildly inaccurate, this picture of the fighting around Hougoumont does convey some feeling of the intensity of the struggle. (Anne S. K. Brown Military Collection, Brown University Library)

they did so the British artillery began to fire on them, but the men of the 1er Léger pushed into the wood, where their numbers again forced the British and German defenders to fall back to the Hougoumont complex.

French artillery also began a bombardment of British positions in and around Hougoumont, which greatly assisted the French infantry assault. In particular, Wellington's infantry positioned on the high ground beyond Hougoumont suffered from the cannon fire. The 23rd Fusiliers, who had already sustained a number of casualties, saw one of their captains killed by a cannonball, after which their commanding officer, Lieutenant-Colonel Sir Henry Ellis, gave the order for the men to lie down in the hope it would afford them some protection.

Wellington had instructed his artillery not to engage in duels with the French artillery. However, having come under a bombardment, the temptation to return fire (in what is termed counter-battery) was very great and the duke's gunners indeed did so. An example of this was Captain Alexander Cavalié Mercer of G Troop, Royal Horse Artillery, who after coming under French artillery fire decided to ignore his commanding officer's instructions and open his own bombardment. However, this had the effect of drawing fire from even more guns of the French artillery, so he quickly ordered his to cease fire.

THE NORTH GATE

The wall to the south of the complex remained firmly in the hands of the defenders, but the French infantry renewed their attack and were able to work their way round the flanks. Soye's men penetrated the Great Orchard, and the British and German troops now positioned there under Lieutenant-Colonel Alexander George Fraser (Lord Saltoun), were forced to retire. However, the advance of Soye's men soon ground to a halt under heavy musket fire.

Shortly after 12:30, over on the western side of Hougoumont, men of the French 1st Brigade had begun to push their way forward over open ground, forcing Wellington's men there to steadily retire. As Cubières' troops made their way around Hougoumont they came to the north gate, where the large wooden doors had remained open in order to allow the defenders to stay in contact with Wellington's line to the rear. The sudden appearance of the French at the north gate came as a shock to the Guards, who began to retreat inside Hougoumont through the gate into the courtyard. It was at this point that a British sergeant, Ralph Fraser of the 3rd Guards, who was still outside, saw Cubières and knocked him off his horse with his halberd. Fraser then mounted the horse and rode

Men of the Coldstream
Guards, the light
companies of which
defended Hougoumont.
(Anne S. K. Brown
Military Collection,
Brown University
Library)

through the gate into the courtyard, and as he did so the defenders closed the
wooden doors behind him. The wounded Cubières managed to get to his feet and
was carried to safety by his men.

Sous-Lieutenant Legros of the 1er Léger, a huge strong man known as
'*l'Enfonceur*' (meaning 'the basher'), was determined to smash his way into
Hougoumont. He grabbed an axe, most likely from a French sapper, and began
hacking at the doors. Eventually he managed to break through the gate, and as it
gave way a number of French soldiers rushed inside. The defenders inside at once
fell back, with some scrambling to the safety of the buildings. For a brief moment
Legros and his men stood in the yard, seemingly alone.

However, the French soldiers soon came under musket fire from the buildings
and Macdonnell, accompanied by a party of his defenders, made for the gate,
which was still relatively intact. The lieutenant-colonel and his men managed to
close the wooden doors, despite other French soldiers attempting to push their
way in from outside. By now Legros and his men were all killed. At 13:15 Sir John
Byng, the commanding officer of the Guards Brigade, ordered a counter-attack

An engraving depicting one of the many French attacks on Hougoumont.

against the French outside Hougoumont, and Jérôme's men began to withdraw in some disorder.

Undeterred, Jérôme immediately ordered another attack, however this time the French brought with them a howitzer that was placed at the edge of the wood. The gun began firing shells into the complex, with many of them landing in the courtyards or on the roofs of the buildings. In response, at 14:00 Lord Saltoun ordered the Grenadier Company of the 3rd Guards to make a rush at bayonet point into the woods in an attempt to put the gun out of action, but they were driven back. In turn a larger counter-attack was launched forty-five minutes later by the Guards under Colonel Francis Hepburn, who managed to push the French from the orchard back into the wood. The fight for Hougoumont, which has been described as a 'battle within a battle', was now sucking in increasing numbers of men from both sides.

4

PHASE 2: D'ERLON'S INFANTRY ATTACK

At 13:00 Maréchal Grouchy, who was some fifteen kilometres to the east of the battlefield of Waterloo, heard the roar of cannon fire. These were the guns of Napoleon's Grande Batterie, which had begun the 'softening up' of Wellington's line in preparation for the infantry assault. The Maréchal was urged by his senior staff to march to the sound of the guns but Grouchy refused; he had his orders from the emperor. The bombardment would last for thirty minutes, after which the four infantry divisions of d'Erlon's I Corps began to advance. The next phase of the battle had begun.

THE GRANDE BATTERIE

The artillery chosen for this task included the twelve-pounder guns of I, II and VI Corps, which deployed forward of the centre of the French line forming the Grande Batterie. In addition a number of six-pounder guns and howitzers were added, bringing the total to around eighty pieces (although this number is disputed among historians). The basic plan was to batter a hole in the Anglo-Allied line, through

Jean-Baptiste Drouet, Comte d'Erlon. It would be d'Erlon's I French Corps that provided the first major assault against the Anglo-Allied line. However, much of it would be thrown back in disorder in the face of the British heavy cavalry attack. (Courtesy of Andrew Field)

French twelve- and six-pounder guns captured during the Battle of Waterloo. Both are now on public display at Fort Nelson, Hampshire, as part of the Royal Armouries collection. (Photos by Mark Simner)

which d'Erlon would push his infantry supported by cavalry. Overall command of the Grande Batterie was given to Maréchal de Camp Jean-Charles Desales.

During the bombardment the guns of the Grande Batterie are said to have occupied what is today known as the Grand Battery Ridge. This strip of high ground was situated roughly halfway between La Belle Alliance and La Haye-Sainte, stretching over 1,000 metres in a north-easterly direction from the Brussels–Genappe–Charleroi road towards Papelotte.

However, it should be noted that the Grande Batterie is another disputed aspect of the battle. Some historians believe the guns did not extend forward of La Belle Alliance, since it would have rendered them vulnerable being so far forward of the French line. This in turn lends weight to another argument that the Grande Batterie did not in fact exist at all. Whatever the truth, we can be safe in the knowledge that Napoleon's artillery at Waterloo was a formidable force.

To counter the French guns, Wellington was adept at using the reverse of slopes to position the bulk of his men out of sight of the enemy, and thus out of sight of their guns. This tactic he again used to great effect at Waterloo and, squinting through their telescopes, the French artillery officers would not have been able to see exactly where most of the duke's men actually were. As such there were few targets on the forward slope for the French gunners to aim at. Coupled with this was the fact the ground was still soft from the heavy rain and as a consequence many of the cannonballs failed to bounce, sinking into the ground instead. That said, the French guns would still have a murderous effect on the Anglo-Allied troops throughout the day.

THE ADVANCE BEGINS

As the guns thundered away, d'Erlon's infantry moved forward from their positions behind the Grand Battery Ridge. In total there were some thirty-three battalions of infantry involved in the attack – totalling around 17,000 men supported by 800 cavalry. For the first part of the advance they would have to struggle through the limbers and wagons that supported the artillery, although it is possible the French gunners left gaps between the guns for the infantry to pass through. Heavy white smoke from the artillery made seeing what lay ahead virtually impossible, and each man simply followed the one in front. Leading the way were the mounted commanding officers of each battalion. The noise of the bombardment was deafening, and for many it would have been very disorientating.

As the divisions reached the Grand Battery Ridge the artillery ceased firing, and once the infantry had pushed through the gun positions they began the process of

French *voltigeur* of the 1er Léger. (Anne
S. K. Brown Military Collection, Brown
University Library)

forming up into columns. With so many men this was not an easy task, and it is
believed to have taken around ten to fifteen minutes to accomplish. As with the
ongoing assault on Hougoumont, the French infantry would deploy their *tirailleurs*
forward of the main force, and in the case of d'Erlon's advance this provided a
dense screen of 3,000 men.

D'Erlon's divisions were to advance in echelon with 1st Division (under
Joachim Jérôme Quiot du Passage) on the left followed on the right in turn by
2nd Division (François-Xavier Donzelot), 3rd Division (Pierre-Louis Binet de
Marcognet) and 4th Division (Pierre François Joseph Durutte). Quiot would be
the first to advance, with one brigade of his division heading for the crest of
Mont-Saint-Jean while the other would begin the struggle for La Haye-Sainte.

THE FIRST ATTACK ON LA HAYE-SAINTE

Wellington had positioned two brigades of German troops along the centre of his line. To the east of the Brussels–Genappe–Charleroi road was Major-General Augustus Frederick Kielmansegge's 1st Hanoverian brigade of five battalions, while to the west was Colonel Christian Friedrich Wilhelm Freiherr von Ompteda's 2nd King's German Legion (KGL) brigade of four battalions, both part of Major-General Charles Alten's 3rd British Infantry Division. Ompteda had placed his 2nd Battalion, which consisted of six weak companies (400 men) under Major Georg Baring, into La Haye-Sainte to garrison it.

Baring's men were green-jacketed riflemen who were armed with the Baker rifle, a far more accurate weapon than the smoothbore muskets carried by much of the duke's infantry. Although more accurate, due to the rifling which made the

Below left: An officer of the 2nd Battalion, King's German Legion, who defended La Haye-Sainte under the command of Major Georg Baring. (Anne S. K. Brown Military Collection, Brown University Library)

Below right: A rifleman of 95th Regiment in 1815. These green-jacketed British light infantrymen carried the Baker rifle, which was a far more accurate weapon than the smoothbore muskets used by most other line regiments. (Anne S. K. Brown Military Collection, Brown University Library)

LA HAYE-SAINTE

The La Haye-Sainte complex consisted of a number of buildings, including a farmhouse, stables, a barn and a piggery. As with Hougoumont, the garrison had fortified the position, but the farmhouse was not to prove as defensible as the château. (One reason for this was due to the fact that the main wooden door of the barn had been broken up for firewood the previous evening.) However, part of the complex benefitted from walls to the east along the Brussels–Genappe–Charleroi road, while there was a kitchen garden to the north and an orchard to the south.

Although not part of La Haye-Sainte itself, there was a sandpit on the opposite side of the road about fifty metres to the north. This feature had also been garrisoned by Wellington with three companies of the 1st Battalion of the 95th Rifles. Like some of their KGL counterparts, the 95th also wore green jackets and carried the Baker rifle.

ball spin in flight, it took longer to load, as the ball had to be forced down the barrel. As such, riflemen were only able to fire on average one round per minute, while those armed with muskets could fire two or even three in the same time.

Two of Quiot's regiments, the 54e and 55e Régiment d'Infanterie de Ligne, reached La Haye-Sainte at about 13:30. The 54e attacked the position through the orchard, while the 55e approached from the west and took the kitchen garden. The orchard had been defended by three companies of the KGL, with a fourth in the garden, leaving the remaining two in the buildings. However, the defenders were quickly forced to abandon both the orchard and garden to seek the safety of the complex itself.

The defenders were able to repulse the French attacks, but three of Baring's officers, including his second-in-command Major Adolphus Bosewiel, were killed and another six wounded. Worried about losing the hard-pressed position, Alten ordered Lieutenant-Colonel August von Klencke's Hanoverian Lüneburg battalion to mount a counter-attack. However, after Klencke moved forward he was himself attacked by French *cuirassiers* (heavy cavalry), who had advanced in support of Quiot's division. Klencke was killed and his men began to run back to the main Anglo-Allied line, although a few would join the defenders in La Haye-Sainte.

An engraving depicting one of the repeated French attacks on La Haye-Sainte.

THE MAIN ADVANCE

Meanwhile, the other divisions of d'Erlon's I Corps had begun their advance, moving off in five-minute intervals from left to right. In front, leading the assault, was Ney on horseback, while behind him the drummers beat their drums and the men shouted '*Vive l'Empereur!*' As the divisions descended down the Grand Battery Ridge and got clear of the guns the Grande Batterie recommenced its bombardment.

Wellington, who had been watching the defence of Hougoumont, quickly realised that something was happening at his centre and galloped over to assess the situation. The Anglo-Allied artillery now opened fire on the advancing French divisions, tearing holes through the dense ranks of men. However, d'Erlon's troops marched on and finally began to move up the forward slope in front of the duke's line.

Few of Wellington's men could be seen by the French soldiers, since most were still hidden on the reverse slope. However, a thin line of Anglo-Allied skirmishers could be spotted steadily retiring in the face of the French advance. In front of Donzelot's 2nd Division was Major-General Willem Frederik van Bijlandt's (mixed Dutch and Belgian) 1st Brigade of Lieutenant-General Henri-Georges

Perponcher-Sedlnitzky's 2nd Netherlands Infantry Division. Bijlandt's brigade, an inexperienced formation that had received its baptism of fire at Quatre-Bras, was deployed in front of the Chemin d'Ohain road on the exposed forward slope under the murderous French artillery fire. This battered brigade was about to face the full onslaught of Donzelot's infantry.

By around 14:00, I Corps was nearing the top of the crest, and as they did so Bijlandt's men delivered a number of volleys into the ranks of the oncoming French infantry. However, the French advance did not falter and four of Bijlandt's five demoralised battalions lost their nerve and broke, leaving a 250-metre gap in Wellington's line.

Lieutenant-General Sir Thomas Picton's 5th British Infantry Division had been on the reverse slope, lying down to avoid the French cannon fire. The 9th Brigade of this division was commanded by Major-General Sir Denis Pack, who had four battalions, including the 3/1st Regiment of Foot (Royal Scots), the 42nd (Black Watch), the 44th (East Essex) and the 92nd (Gordon Highlanders). Moments after Bijlandt's men left their positions Pack's men stood up, and a vicious firefight with the French commenced. It was here that Picton, while attempting to rally his men, was killed by a musket ball that penetrated his top hat.

INTERVENTION OF THE BRITISH HEAVY CAVALRY

At this crucial point of the battle, around 14:20, Lieutenant-General Henry Paget (Earl of Uxbridge) gave orders to his Household and Union brigades to mount a charge. Up until this point this heavy cavalry had been on the reverse slope of Mont-Saint-Jean and unseen by the French.

As the Household Brigade reached the crest the French came into view, and the sixteen-year-old trumpeter John Edwards sounded the charge. By this time there was only a short distance between the British cavalry and the French *cuirassiers*, but since they were moving down the slope the horses managed to get up some speed. The British heavies crashed into the French *cuirassiers* and a short but ferocious struggle began just to the west of La Haye-Sainte. The clatter of sword on sword and sword on breastplate (worn by the *cuirassiers*) rang out across that part of the battlefield, in what Somerset later described as 'so many tinkers at work'.

However, this clash of the heavies was short-lived, and within two or three minutes the French cavalrymen withdrew, leaving Somerset to begin a pursuit.

Lieutenant-General Sir Thomas Picton, who was killed when commanding the 5th British Infantry Division at Waterloo. Wellington said he was as 'rough, foul-mouthed a devil as ever lived'. (Anne S. K. Brown Military Collection, Brown University Library)

BRITISH HOUSEHOLD AND UNION BRIGADES

At Waterloo, the British had two heavy cavalry brigades with a combined force of approximately 2,600 sabres. The 1st British (Household) Cavalry Brigade was commanded by Major-General Lord Edward Somerset and consisted of the 1st and 2nd Life Guards, the Royal Horse Guards (The Blues) and the 1st (King's) Dragoon Guards. The 2nd British (Union) Cavalry Brigade was commanded by Major-General Sir William Ponsonby and consisted of the 1st (Royal) Dragoons, the 2nd Royal North Dragoons (Scots Greys) and the 6th (Inniskilling) Dragoons. At the time Uxbridge gave the order to advance, the Household Brigade was deployed behind the Anglo-Allied line on the western side of the Brussels–Genappe–Charleroi road while the Union Brigade was on the eastern side.

Troopers of the British Household Cavalry in 1815. (Anne S. K. Brown Military Collection, Brown University Library)

Right: An officer of the Royal North British Dragoons in 1815, more commonly known as the Scots Greys. (Anne S. K. Brown Military Collection, Brown University Library)

Below: The Second Life Guards at Waterloo, who fought a short but fierce contest with French *cuirassiers* during the charge of the British heavy cavalry. (Anne S. K. Brown Military Collection, Brown University Library)

Some of the *cuirassiers* ended caught up among their own infantry along the sunken lane. Here they came under fire from the 95th Rifles.

Meanwhile the Union Brigade had pushed through their own infantry lines and the Royal Dragoons hacked their way into Charles-Francois Bourgeois' 2nd Infantry Brigade of Quiot's 1st Infantry Division, during which the eagle of the 105e Ligne was captured. The Inniskillings likewise smashed their way into Donzelot's division, while the Scots Greys, who were supposed to have remained in reserve but did not want to miss their chance to take part in the action, hit Marcognet's division and captured the eagle of the 45e Ligne. The latter eagle was taken by Sergeant Charles Ewart, who would later be promoted to ensign for his efforts.

Napoleon allegedly referred to the Scots Greys as '*Ces terribles chevaux gris*' during their attack on Marcognet's 3rd French Infantry Division. (Anne S. K. Brown Military Collection, Brown University Library)

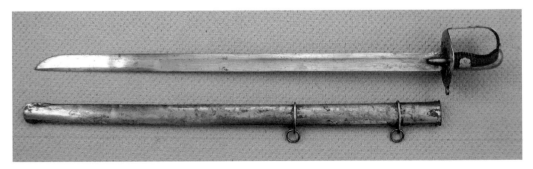

British 1796 Pattern Heavy Cavalry Sword used by the Household and Union brigades. (Author's collection)

THE COUNTER-ATTACK OF THE FRENCH CAVALRY

At the point of almost defeat Uxbridge had saved the day, routing much of d'Erlon's I Corps and sending it reeling back to the French lines. Only Durutte's division had been able to form squares (a tactic used by infantry to fend off cavalry) and conduct an orderly withdrawal. However, the blood was up for the men of the Household and Union brigades, who now turned their attention to the Grande Batterie while others headed for the French line. A number of officers attempted to regain control of their men in order to regroup and retire, but their efforts would be in vain.

A member of the 1er Régiment des Chevaux-Légers. It would be French light cavalry such as this that would carry out the devastating counter-attack on the British Household and Union brigades. (Anne S. K. Brown Military Collection, Brown University Library)

Sir William Ponsonby, who was killed while attempting to rally his men against the counter-attack of the French cavalry. (Anne S. K. Brown Military Collection, Brown University Library)

By the time the two brigades reached the French guns their horses were blown, having exerted most of their energy in the short, sharp fighting moments before. To the horror of the British cavalrymen, they now came under attack from the French cavalry, including *cuirassiers* from Édouard Jean-Baptiste Milhaud's IV Cavalry Corps and *lanciers* from Charles Claude Jacquinot's 1st Cavalry Division.

Ponsonby attempted to rally his men to fight off the French cavalry, but was killed. Many of the British heavy cavalry tried to make it back to their lines, but their exhausted horses were easily caught up by the relatively fresh French horses. The *cuirassiers* and *lanciers* pursued, killing and wounding many of the British cavalrymen, resulting in the loss of over 1,200 men and 1,300 horses – some 46–48 per cent of their overall strength.

5

PHASE 3: NEY'S CAVALRY ATTACKS

Prior to d'Erlon's ill-fated advance Napoleon had been surveying the battlefield through his telescope, and as he did so something in the distance to the right caught his attention. The emperor passed the telescope to Soult and asked him what he thought it was. Soult cast his eye through the telescope, after which he turned to the emperor and told him that it was troops on the move. Other officers also took a look; some concurred with Soult and stated that they believed they were heading in their direction.

FRENCH BLUE OR PRUSSIAN BLACK?

Soult suggested that the troops were Grouchy's, but Napoleon ordered his 3rd and 5th cavalry divisions, under Généraux de Division Jean Simon Domon and Jacques Gervais Subervie respectively, to provide additional cover on his right flank. Whether the emperor considered these mysterious troops as a threat or believed it was Grouchy remains unclear, but Domon appears to have believed the battle was already won and that his orders were to link up with Grouchy.

What Napoleon in fact saw were Prussian troops of General Freidrich Wilhelm Bülow von Dennewitz's IV Army Corps marching to Wellington's assistance. Any doubt the emperor had about the troop movement quickly disappeared when a Prussian prisoner was brought before him. The Prussian informed his captors that not only were the advancing figures Bülow's men, but that the entire Prussian army was making its way from Wavre, where it had not at all been molested by the French.

Meanwhile Wellington was anxiously waiting for the Prussians and, despite having received word earlier in the day that Bülow's corps was getting close, the wait seemed an agonising one. The advance of the Prussians was proving difficult, the primitive roads having suffered heavily during the rain of the night. The men of IV Corps were also exhausted, having been on an almost constant march for the past three days; they had also had to overcome various obstacles such as swollen rivers and dense woods, not to mention the narrow congested streets of Wavre. Yet despite all this the Prussians pushed on, determined to honour Blücher's promise to come to the duke's aid.

NAPOLEON'S REACTION

There has been much debate among historians as to the emperor's reaction upon hearing the news of the Prussian approach. Indeed, he himself stated in his memoirs that he had ordered Lobau's VI Corps to hold up the Prussians on his right flank. However, the emperor's claims have to be treated with suspicion, since he was prone to exaggeration and often changed the facts to fit his arguments. Général de Division Jean-Baptiste Jeanin, who commanded the 20th Infantry Division, believed VI Corps' objective was to support the attack on the centre of the Anglo-Allied line. Jeanin also later stated that as soon as they saw the Prussians pouring out of the wood, which had come as a complete surprise, his corps received new orders to reposition to meet the threat.

It has also been argued that Napoleon was under the belief that Grouchy would arrive in time to attack the Prussians. At 10:00 the emperor had sent a message to the Maréchal asking him to enter his sphere of operations, but Grouchy did not receive this until 16:00. Nor did he receive a second message despatched to him at 13:00, which ordered him to march towards La Belle Alliance, until some six hours later. As such, Napoleon was expecting Grouchy to come to his aid, yet the Maréchal was still following his original orders to pursue the Prussians. General Étienne Maurice Gérard implored him to march to the sounds of the guns but Grouchy refused.

After the battle Grouchy would be blamed for his emperor's defeat and would spend much of the rest of his life defending himself. To this day historians continue to debate the issue, but on 18 June 1815 Napoleon would not be able to benefit from the additional men and guns under Grouchy's command.

THE FRENCH CAVALRY ATTACK

At 16:00 the battle entered its next phase, that of the massed French cavalry attacks against the Anglo-Allied army. Earlier Ney had ordered a renewed infantry assault against La Haye-Sainte (see below), and as he strained to view what was going on through the heavy smoke he saw what he believed to be units of Wellington's army making a withdrawal. At this the Maréchal wrongly assumed his enemy's line was beginning to buckle, when in fact the duke was merely moving some of his men back to the safety of the reverse slope while the wounded and prisoners were also being moved to the rear.

Over on the Anglo-Allied side the senior officers realised that the French were preparing what looked like an advance of cavalry in force. The French cavalry units detailed for the initial attack included Edouard Jean Baptiste Milhaud's IV Reserve Cavalry Corps and Charles Lefebvre-Desnouettes' Garde Impériale Light Cavalry Division. Combined, these consisted of ten cavalry regiments, or some 4,400 sabres.

Another Waterloo-related debate among historians is whether Napoleon authorised the cavalry attacks at this juncture of the battle or whether Ney simply took it upon himself to carry them out. The emperor certainly attempted to distance himself from the decision after the battle, but again Napoleon's words

Although dated 1812, these charging *cuirassiers* show how formidable the French cavalry must have appeared to the Anglo-Allies at Waterloo. (Anne S. K. Brown Military Collection, Brown University Library)

cannot always be trusted. It does seem odd that the movement of so many men on horses would have gone unnoticed by the emperor, and it is possible that not knowing the dispositions and strength of Wellington's forces on the reverse slope led him to make an error of judgement.

Ney, who was known affectionately as '*le Rougeaud*' (meaning redhead or ginger) by his men on account of the colour of his hair, had no hesitation in personally leading the attack. And at around 16:00 the first wave formed up and began their advance towards the Anglo-Allied line. The advance of the French cavalry was funnelled between Hougoumont and La Haye-Sainte, in a gap of no more than 950 metres. Through this gap the *cuirassiers* moved up the forward slope of Mont-Saint-Jean. As they arrived at the top of the crest Wellington's main force now became visible and what they saw before them on the reverse slope were several dozen infantry squares.

INFANTRY SQUARES

Forming square was a tactic used by the infantry to protect themselves against cavalry. Usually the square would, as the name suggests, have four sides, each of which was formed by four ranks of men. The first two ranks would be kneeling with their muskets, bayonets fixed, pointing upwards at roughly a forty-five-degree angle with the butts resting on the ground. This would present the enemy cavalry a hedge of steel spikes, which horses were understandably reluctant to impale themselves upon. The rear two ranks would be standing, a position from which they were able to deliver volleys of fire into the enemy. The usual tactic was to fire on the horses rather than the men since a dismounted *cuirassier*, weighed down by his heavy armour, was virtually useless on foot. Other troops, such as artillerymen, could seek sanctuary in the interior of a square, providing they could reach one in time. The main disadvantage of the square was the fact it was particularly vulnerable to artillery fire.

Opposite top: British India Pattern 'Brown Bess' Musket, the standard muzzle-loading smoothbore weapon carried by most British infantrymen throughout the Napoleonic Wars. (Author's collection)

Opposite bottom: As with most muskets of the day, the 'Brown Bess' used a flintlock ignition system that was prone to misfires if the black powder became damp. (Author's collection)

There was little else the French cavalry could do but push on and attempt to break the squares, an extremely difficult task if the infantrymen held firm. For the Anglo-Allied troops the sight of the French cavalry, probably the best in the world at that time, was a fearsome one. Indeed, when the enemy appeared on the crest the young and inexperienced troops of Wellington's army were extremely alarmed. When ordered to open fire many fired high, missing their targets due to the panic they were experiencing. However, they still managed to hold their ground.

According to Ensign Rees Howell Gronow, who was inside a square of the 3/1st Foot Guards, 'The horses of the first rank of Cuirassiers, in spite of all the efforts of their riders, came to a standstill, shaking and covered with foam, at about twenty yards distance, and generally resisted all attempts to force them to charge the line of serried steel.' Unable to break the squares, some of the French cavalry turned their attention to Wellington's artillery, which they soon overwhelmed.

For the next two hours the French cavalry would attempt to charge Wellington's squares before withdrawing, after which they would return and charge again. Ney would commit further cavalry units to the ongoing attack, with some twenty regiments totalling almost 9,000 men being engaged in the assault at some point until it finally came to an end just before 18:00. The Maréchal himself had three horses shot from under him during the course of this part of the afternoon.

Ultimately the French cavalry attacks failed for two main reasons. Firstly Ney's men did not spike the Anglo-Allied guns they overran, which meant Wellington's most destructive form of firepower was soon back in action. Secondly Napoleon did not provide infantry support for his cavalry, and if he had sent in his reserves the ridge of Mont-Saint-Jean, and much of the artillery along it, would likely have fallen into French hands. Ney did eventually order Gilbert Desiré Bachelu's 5th and Foy's 9th infantry divisions to advance, but by the time he did so it was

Ney's cavalry charge at Waterloo. The repeated charges lasted for almost two hours, yet failed to break the Anglo-Allied squares. (Anne S. K. Brown Military Collection, Brown University Library)

too late. Most of the French cavalrymen and horses were now exhausted and could not support an infantry assault. However, the cavalry attacks did have the effect of putting Wellington's centre under extreme pressure.

THE FALL OF LA HAYE-SAINTE

Just before the commencement of the French cavalry attacks, Ney had ordered a renewed assault on the position of La Haye-Sainte at around 15:00. During the thirty-minute lull the defenders of the farm had set about reorganising the defence and a number of reinforcements, including two companies of the 1st Light Battalion of the KGL under the command of Captains Frederick von Gilsa and Henry Marschalk, were sent to assist. These reinforcements were ordered to take up defensive positions in the garden while the original defenders held the buildings. However, the orchard was abandoned.

The assault was again made by Colonel Claude Charlet's men of the 54e and 55e Ligne, who managed to virtually surround La Haye-Sainte. The French assaulted the walls and the buildings from which the defenders fired through their loopholes. Perhaps the most heavily contested section of the defence was the gate by the barn, although the attackers continued to probe all possible entrances. A company of the 5th Line Battalion of the KGL was also sent in to reinforce the garrison, but as it advanced its commanding officer, Captain Ernest Christian Charles von Wurmb, was killed by cannon fire. Unlike the men of the Light Battalion, the 5th Line wore red coats and carried smoothbore muskets. Ompteda would also be killed while attempting to counter-attack the French.

When the French cavalry attacks began, Baring's riflemen opened fire on the *cuirassiers*, causing a number of casualties. As 17:00 approached the French attack began to ease, but the defenders were now severely short of rifle ammunition. Despite several appeals for resupply, none arrived, although about 150 men of the 1st Battalion of the 2nd Nassau Regiment did manage to make their way in to bolster the defence. With them the Nassauers had brought large metal kettles, which became extremely useful when the French set the barn roof on fire, being used to carry water to put it out.

At 18:00 another lull in the fighting came, but Baring realised that his men were now on the verge of defeat. He estimated that only around three or four rounds per man were left, and coupled with the number of casualties and tiredness of his troops there was little hope of holding on for much longer. The major again sent a request for ammunition, but again none arrived. Within thirty minutes the French renewed their assault and it would be the men of Colonel Gougeon's 13e Léger, from Donzelot's division, that carried out the attack.

This time the French infantry managed to smash their way through the stables into the complex, but the defenders drove them off at bayonet point. Yet again Baring requested more ammunition, but yet again none was forthcoming. The French were now on the roof of the stable firing down into the defenders below who, out of ammunition, could not return fire. The door leading to the Brussels–Genappe–Charleroi road was also smashed through by Lieutenant Vieux who, like Legros at Hougoumont, used an axe to gain entrance. Unable to hold the position any longer, Baring ordered the surviving defenders to retire through the garden, from where they made their way back to the main Anglo-Allied Line. La Haye-Sainte was now in French hands.

THE SITUATION AT HOUGOUMONT

Meanwhile the battle for Hougoumont was continuing with great ferocity. The emperor had been forced to order more troops to assist in the attack, which were to be provided by Général de Brigade Baron Toussaint Campi's 2nd Brigade of the 5th Division deployed near La Belle Alliance. As they moved towards Hougoumont the Anglo-Allied artillery did much damage to their ranks, with Campi's formation breaking up and being driven back before reaching the orchard.

The French then brought into action a battery of howitzers, which began firing incendiary shells into Hougoumont. This artillery attack resulted in the château, the chapel and the great barn being set alight, and a desperate attempt was made to rescue the wounded who had been placed in the buildings. Not all would be removed to safety before the fire made further attempts impossible.

Seeing the flames, Wellington sent orders that the position was still to be defended, and the Guards and Nassauers remained at their posts fending off their attackers. Thankfully for the defenders a resupply of ammunition had made its way into Hougoumont via the north gate between 15:00 and 16:00. At this point, as Ney began his cavalry attacks, there was a lull in the fighting around Hougoumont, but the struggle for the complex was not to end yet.

6

PHASE 4: ARRIVAL OF THE PRUSSIANS

With the imminent loss of La Haye-Sainte, the growing pressure on Hougoumont and the seemingly relentless cavalry attacks, the situation for Wellington was beginning to look bleak. Although the British heavy cavalry had set about killing as many French gunners as they could find during their ill-fated attack on the Grande Batterie, Napoleon had promptly begun to reconstitute his artillery by using infantry to assist the surviving artillerymen and reinforcing it with guns of the Garde Impériale. The guns were brought back into action so quickly that it is said many on the Allied side of the line had not noticed the break in the bombardment.

WELLINGTON'S CRITICAL MOMENT

Wellington was well aware that the French reserves still offered the emperor a formidable force with which to finally smash his line. Indeed, the duke's line was growing ever weaker, with Picton's 5th and Alten's 3rd infantry divisions, the former still reeling at the death of their commander and the latter having borne the brunt of the French artillery attacks, in rather poor shape. Wellington had little choice but to commit his own reserves by pushing them forward to reinforce his battered line.

Now facing the rear of La Haye-Sainte was Major-General Sir John Lambert's 10th Brigade of the 6th Infantry Division, which included three veteran regiments that had seen action in North America during the War of 1812. These included 4th, 27th and 40th regiments of foot. Similarly, Major-General August von Kruse's Nassau Brigade was ordered forward to take up positions to the right near Kielmansegge's brigade. Other reserves were moved towards the right flank near Hougoumont, including Lieutenant-Colonel George Charles du Plat's 1st KGL Brigade and Colonel Elias Olfermann's Brunswick's Division. The former would send his light companies into Hougoumont, while the latter would take up positions on the high ground behind the complex.

A grenadier of the 40th Regiment of Foot as he would have appeared in 1815. This regiment was one of the few veteran British units at Waterloo, having seen service in North America during the War of 1812. (Anne S. K. Brown Military Collection, Brown University Library)

By 16:00 Wellington had sixty of his eighty-three battalions in line, of which seventeen had suffered heavily during the fighting so far. Napoleon on the other hand had 103 battalions, of which only fifty-seven had been actively involved in the battle. Of the forty-six uncommitted battalions, twenty-two were of the elite Garde Impériale. It is, therefore, perhaps unsurprising that while an air of pessimism descended over the Allied commanders, the emperor remained relatively optimistic. However, that was about to change!

BLÜCHER ARRIVES!

The battle now entered its fourth phase with the arrival of the Prussian army. Advanced units of Blücher's force had been watching the battle for several hours from the Bois de Paris, eyeing up the French army while waiting for their own to catch up. A group of *uhlans* (Prussian cavalry) under Major von Falkenhausen had even managed to get behind Napoleon's rear south of La Belle Alliance. After taking several French soldiers and a local farmer prisoner, it appeared to the Prussians that both the village of Lasne and the Bois de Paris were devoid of any French troops.

Having penetrated the unprotected wood, the recently arrived Blücher, accompanied by Bülow and August Neidhardt von Gneisenau, Blücher's chief of staff, was able to study the deployment of the French unmolested. Although this incredible stroke of luck much assisted the Prussians in their planning for the coming attack, the sight of the famed Garde Impériale would not have filled them with much joy at the prospect of meeting them in battle.

Gebhard Leberecht von Blücher, Fürst von Wahlstatt, who despite being beaten at Ligny was determined to come to Wellington's aid at Waterloo. It was the timely arrival of the Prussian army that tipped the balance in favour of the Allies and ensured victory. (Rijksmuseum)

Much of Bülow's IV Corps was soon in or near the wood and, although some units had not yet caught up, Blücher decided he could delay no longer since it appeared to him that Wellington had now reached his most critical moment of the battle. The first Prussian troops began to pour out of the wood at around 16:30, and upon seeing them, the French senior staff quickly realised that their right flank was in serious danger.

Prussian cavalry clashed with those of Domon and Subervie, and despite initial success for the French light cavalry, they were soon forced to withdraw under fire from Prussian artillery positioned on the edge of the wood. With the way now clear, Prussian skirmishers were able to fan out and begin their advance. Although Wellington had hoped the Prussians would make contact with his left flank, the fall of La Haye-Sainte had prompted them to head south-west instead.

As such, the Prussian advance would come into contact with Lobau's VI Corps, but this force could not withstand the superior numbers of relatively fresh Prussian infantry and cavalry arrayed against him. Lobau ordered a withdrawal towards the village of Plancenoit, which appeared to be the objective of the Prussians, while Domon and Subervie did their best to slow the Prussian advance by mounting several charges. However, the Prussian advance was now unstoppable, and fire from their artillery was even hitting the inn at La Belle Alliance.

Blücher leading Prussian troops at Waterloo. Although seventy-two years of age, the Prussian *feldmarschall* often led from the front, including in a cavalry charge at Ligny where his horse was shot from under him. (The British Library Board)

THE STRUGGLE FOR PLANCENOIT

Much has been written about the fighting for Hougoumont and La Haye-Sainte since the Battle of Waterloo ended. However, the equally important struggle for Plancenoit has, at least until more recent years, been largely relegated to a sideshow. Yet, as important as Hougoumont and La Haye-Sainte were, Plancenoit also played an important part in the Allies' eventual victory over Napoleon.

Plancenoit was the largest of the inhabited areas within the confines of the Waterloo battlefield, being a village in the proper sense of the word complete with square and a church. Here some of the French soldiers had spent the night sheltering from the rain, and most of the wooden shutters had been burnt as firewood. Wisely the residents had abandoned their homes the day before the battle, so when Prussian and French troops clashed, in what was some of the bitterest fighting of the day, the village was deserted.

Realising that holding Plancenoit was critical, the emperor ordered Général de Division Guillaume Philibert Duhesme's Young Guard to move into the village and defend it. This was something Napoleon was reluctant to do since he needed all his Garde Impériale to conduct the final blow against Wellington. However, there was realistically little else he could redeploy in time to reinforce Lobau's VI Corps, which was now in danger of being overwhelmed.

When the two opposing forces clashed in and around Plancenoit, the Prussian hatred of the French ensured the fighting would be both violent and bloody. The contest took the form of street fighting, with houses being captured, lost and recaptured. Little mercy was shown by either side, but the inexperienced Prussian infantry, many of them young and poorly trained, mounted weak attacks that were beaten off by the more experienced French. Some Prussian skirmishers facing Lobau's infantry even attempted to give up entirely and began a hasty withdrawal, only to come into contact with their own cavalry who compelled them to return to the fight. Yet despite this, Duhesme and Lobau made little headway themselves in the face of the Prussian onslaught.

The Prussian 16th Infantry Brigade under Colonel Hiller von Gärtringen did manage to fight its way into the village square, where they came face-to-face with Duhesme's Young Guard. A somewhat confused fight then took place, but the French got the upper hand and began to drive the Prussians out of the village. Seeing this, a furious Blücher forced his way on horseback through the disordered troops to find Hiller, and once he did so he impressed upon the colonel the absolute importance of taking Plancenoit. It was at this moment, while Hiller

Prussian and French infantry clash during the vicious struggle for Plancenoit. (Anne S. K. Brown Military Collection, Brown University Library)

attempted to rally his men, word reached Blücher of news from Johann von Thielemann that the Prussian troops still at Wavre were under attack. Grouchy had begun the final major action of the Hundred Days campaign, the Battle of Wavre. However, Blücher knew he could not abandon his position at Waterloo in order to assist.

Although Wellington was aware something was happening at Plancenoit – he could see smoke rising above it – he did not know exactly what was taking place. However, what the unseen battle was doing was drawing away vitally important men from the emperor's reserve, which now could not be used against the Anglo-Allies.

BLÜCHER ATTACKS AGAIN

Despite their initial repulse the Prussians quickly planned to assault Plancenoit again, and this time the attack was to be conducted by Major Count von

Reichenbach of the 11th Infantry Brigade. Unlike Hiller's men, those of the 11th were steadier in battle and their assault had the desired effect of pushing Duhesme's men back. Bitter house-to-house fighting again raged in the village, much of it using the bayonet or musket butt. Again the Prussians reached the village square, only again to be driven out.

At this point in the battle Major-General Georg Dubislav Ludwig von Pirch's II Corps was beginning to arrive, which encouraged Blücher to order yet another assault on the village. At that, both the 14th and 16th brigades fought their way back in to Plancenoit; this time Duhesme was wounded in the head and the defence of the Young Guard finally began to falter. Some members of the Guard even attempted to surrender, but those who did found themselves on the receiving end of Prussian bayonets.

The emperor had been busy organising the remainder of his reserve, which included the thirteen battalions of the Middle and Old Guard, but he was now in a dilemma. He desperately needed his reserve to make the final thrust against Wellington, but he also could not afford to let the Prussians break through on his right flank. Faced with this difficult decision, Napoleon ordered part of his reserves to leave the main assault force destined for the Anglo-Allied line, and redeployed them over on his right flank in square formation. He also ordered two Old Guard battalions, the 1/2e Grenadiers à Pied under Major François Martenot and 1/2e Chasseurs à Pied under Major Jacques Colomban, to retake the village.

The Old Guard battalions marched into battle and lived up to their reputation of being both elite and ruthless. Although heavily outnumbered by the Prussians (the two battalions combined amounted to little more than 1,000 men), they drove their enemy out of the village in less than twenty minutes. Prussian prisoners, like their Young Guard foes earlier, were afforded little quarter. It was now 19:30 and Blücher had once again failed to break the emperor's right flank.

ZIETEN'S I CORPS

Although Wellington could not see the fighting in Plancenoit, he could see other Prussian troops arriving over on his left flank near the hamlet of Papelotte. These men were of Hans Ernst Karl, Graf von Zieten's I Corps, which had marched from Wavre along a more northerly route to that of Bülow's IV Corps. As they came into view Karl Freiherr von Müffling, the Prussian liaison officer attached to Wellington's army, made his way over to greet the advanced guard, where he informed Lieutenant-Colonel von Reiche that Wellington was on the verge of being compelled to begin a withdrawal.

Zieten, however, was reluctant to commit his troops to form up with the Anglo-Allied army, since it appeared to him he would be marching into the middle of a defeat. A request also reached the I Corps commander from Bülow who, struggling to break through at Plancenoit, desperately needed assistance. Müffling pleaded with Zieten, stating that should they fail to come to the duke's aid they would have broken Blücher's promise in the eyes of Wellington since he was unaware of what was happening in Plancenoit. At that Zieten issued orders for I Corps to march to assist the duke.

Zieten's men would clash with Durutte's 4th Infantry Division around Papelotte. The French troops in this part of battlefield had been putting pressure on the Nassauers holding Papelotte, La Haye, Smohain and Fischermont. However, the sudden arrival of the Prussian I Corps saw the French become hopelessly outnumbered. Indeed, Durutte's division was much reduced, having previously detached one of his two brigades to assist in the assault against La Haye-Sainte. Initially the French put up a determined fight, but as increasing numbers of Prussians poured into the fight Durutte's men were eventually forced to begin a withdrawal.

August Neidhard von Gneisenau, who acted as chief of staff to Blücher. Prior to Waterloo he had been instrumental in the reform of the Prussian army following defeats earlier in the Napoleonic Wars. (Anne S. K. Brown Military Collection, Brown University Library)

7

PHASE 5: ATTACK OF THE GARDE IMPÉRIALE

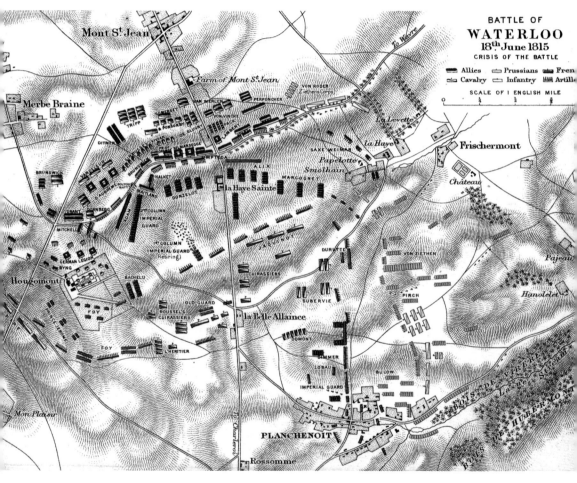

A Battle of Waterloo map showing deployment of the armies during Wellington's crisis of the battle.

Although Wellington's Anglo-Allied army was at breaking point, the arrival of the Prussians on to the field had tipped the balance into his favour. It was time for Napoleon to make his final throw of the dice; it was time to commit his famed Garde Impériale. However, before describing the events of this final stage of the battle it should be understood that a number of different interpretations of the attack exist. As such, the following is just one view and the reader should also explore others.

THE GARDE IMPÉRIALE

The Garde Impériale is probably the most well-known military formation of the Napoleonic Wars. Its roots can be found in the Gardes des Consuls (Consular Guard), which had previously fought with Napoleon during the French Revolutionary Wars, and had been present at the Battle of Marengo in 1800. These guardsmen were already considered an elite, being tall, literate (at a time when illiteracy was high) and required to have seen action in at least three campaigns before becoming eligible to join.

In 1804 the emperor transformed the Gardes des Consuls into the Garde Impériale, and in 1810 he divided them into three parts, including the Old, Middle and Young Guard. The Old Guard were the most experienced veterans of Napoleon's earliest campaigns, while the Middle Guard were men who had seen action between 1805 and 1809. The Young Guard, however, were made up of the best recruits from the more recent intake of conscripts and volunteers, and as such were never considered as good as the other two.

By the time of the Battle of Waterloo, the Garde Impériale had a fearsome reputation for being brutal in battle. They were often despised by other French soldiers, possibly due to their brutality and additional privileges, yet many also desired to become one of them. The Garde Impériale included infantry, cavalry and artillery, which the emperor usually kept in reserve until, sensing victory, he unleased them during the final moments of the battle.

THE FINAL ATTACK

Napoleon personally led the Garde Impériale to within 500 metres of La Haye-Sainte on the western side of the Brussels–Genappe–Charleroi road. Here they would form up for the final attack, and their distinctive music could be heard drifting across the battlefield. Wellington would have been left in no doubt

An ensign of grenadiers of the Garde Impériale. (Anne S. K. Brown Military Collection, Brown University Library)

about what was to happen next. The emperor continued with them until just before reaching the orchard of La Haye-Sainte, where he turned back, handing command of the assault to Ney.

In total there would be nine battalions of the Garde Impériale committed for the attack, including six of the Middle Guard – consisting of the 1/3e and 2/3e grenadiers, the 1/3e and 2/3e chasseurs, and a battalion of each of the 4e Grenadiers and 4e Chasseurs. These would be followed by three of the Old Guard – consisting of the 2/1er Chasseurs, 1/2e Grenadiers and 2/2e Chasseurs. The formation would advance in two echelons, with the Middle Guard leading, followed by the Old Guard. A horse artillery battery, under Lieutenant-Colonel Jean-Baptiste Duchand de Sancey, would also accompany the former. There is a difference of opinion between historians about how the Garde Impériale conducted their advance, some arguing they marched in columns while others believe it was in squares. Indeed, witnesses on both sides of the battle do not agree.

Despite popular myth, the Garde Impériale did not carry out the final assault alone. They were joined by Donzelot's Division on the right, and orders were sent to d'Erlon and Reille to also exert pressure on the Anglo-Allied line. Cavalry would also be used to support the assault. It is alleged that the emperor instructed Général de Division Pierre François Marie Auguste Dejean and Maréchal de Camp Charles de la Bédoyère to inform the divisions that the sound of firing over on the right flank was Grouchy engaging the Prussians. A lie he hoped would keep up morale until the attack succeeded, by which time it would be too late for the Prussians to help the duke.

The advance began at 19:30, the light of the day already having begun to fade, and again the attack would be made against the centre right of Wellington's line. The duke had already set about reinforcing his front, placing Major-General Sir John Vandeleur's 4th and Major-General Sir Hussey Vivian's 6th cavalry brigades, both of light cavalry, along his centre and right. He deployed Lieutenant-General Baron David-Hendrik Chassé's 3rd Netherlands Infantry Division, which consisted of twelve battalions, behind Major-General Peregrine Maitland's 1st Guards Brigade, also on the right. Also arrayed against the Garde Impériale was Major-General Sir Colin Halkett's 5th Infantry Brigade to Maitland's left, while the Brunswick, KGL, Nassau and Hanoverian formations near La Haye-Sainte would face Donzelot's advance.

The Garde Impériale advanced towards the Anglo-Allied lines virtually unmolested, since Wellington's gunners were now either wounded or exhausted as well as low on ammunition. However, it is said Captain Carel Frederik Krahmer de Bichin's Belgian battery did manage to open fire on the French troops advancing in front of Maitland's position. Despite this, the men of the Middle Guard marched on, and soon came within musket range of Maitland's two battalions of 1st Foot Guards. Donzelot had also pushed his way forward and had come into contact with the Brunswick and Nassau troops, the latter of which, under Kruse, managed to drive back its French adversaries.

Meanwhile, the Middle Guard 4e and 1/3e Grenadiers à Pied, under majors Lafargue and Guillemin respectively, came up against Halkett's 30th, 33rd,

Nassau infantry advancing during the latter stages of the Battle of Waterloo. (Anne S. K. Brown Military Collection, Brown University Library)

69th and 73rd regiments of foot. These four regiments had suffered so heavily at Quatre-Bras that they had to join together in order to form two squares. As the Middle Guard came into sight a volley was fired from one of the faces of the squares, after which the British infantrymen were ordered to form a four-man-deep line. The Middle Guard fired their own volley and Halkett's men returned fire with another. Chassé now ordered his guns, under Major Jacques Louis Dominique van der Smissen, to advance and open fire, after which Colonel Hendrik Detmer's 1st Brigade of the 3rd Netherlands Division began to advance. The mounting casualties and sight of Chassé's men proved too much for the 1/3e Grenadiers, who began to break.

Baron David Hendrik Chassé, who commanded the 3rd Netherlands Division at Waterloo. Chassé previously fought with the French earlier in the Napoleonic Wars. (Rijksmuseum)

Kruse's Nassauers, despite having fended off Donzelot's men and begun an advance of their own, were gripped with panic and started to retire. Halkett's four battalions, which likewise had advanced after seeing the Middle Guard retreating down the slope, were given orders to turn around and march back to their original positions. As they did so, Duchand's horse artillery battery opened fire on them, causing heavy casualties, which was followed by panic as the men, now all mixed together, tried desperately to reach cover. For the next five minutes Halkett's brigade was in chaos until a semblance of order could be regained.

Opposite Maitland's 1st Guards Brigade came the 1/3e and 2/3e Chasseurs under majors Cardinal and Angelet. As the two battalions advanced they came under case shot fire from the Anglo-Allied artillery, which caused heavier casualties than those suffered by the grenadiers. Neither could see Maitland's guardsmen through the heavy smoke, and as they reached the crest there was still no sign of their enemy. At that moment Wellington shouted, 'Now Maitland! Now's your time!', and the men of the 1st Foot Guards rose up from where they had been lying on the ground out of sight. As they did so they delivered a devastating volley into the ranks of the *chasseurs*. Both Cardinal and Angelet were hit, as were some twenty other officers and an estimated 300 of their men.

With the loss of so many of their officers, the 1/3e and 2/3e Chasseurs came to a halt and there appeared much confusion among the ranks. Then they began to disintegrate as Maitland's guardsmen charged downhill towards them with bayonets fixed. However, the British guardsmen were soon forced to retire themselves as the 4e Chasseurs under Major Agnès, who had been obscured by smoke, now came into view. Although Maitland attempted to conduct an orderly withdrawal, the retirement turned into confusion as the guardsmen hurried back to their original positions.

Encouraged by the retirement of the British guardsmen, Agnès pushed on and opened fire on an Anglo-Allied battery. Seeing this, Colonel John Colborne of the 52nd Regiment of Foot ordered his skirmishers forward, upon which the 4e Chasseurs similarly opened fire, but as the skirmishers fell back a devastating volley ripped into the ranks of the French formation. This fire had come from the main body of the veteran 52nd Foot, and it cost Agnès his life. The 4e Chasseurs attempted to deploy into line to respond, but after a few minutes they broke and began to retire.

The three remaining battalions of the Old Guard had also begun a withdrawal, and as they did so they would be pursued by British infantry. It was during this retirement that Maréchal de Camp Pierre Jacques Étienne Cambronne allegedly replied when asked to surrender, 'The Guard dies, but does not surrender!' It

French horse artillery of the Garde Impériale attacked by British infantry during Napoleon's last throw of the dice. (Anne S. K. Brown Military Collection, Brown University Library)

is highly unlikely such a verbal exchange took place, and indeed Cambronne later denied he said these words. Whatever the truth, the Old Guard put up a remarkable resistance despite the extremely difficult circumstances in which they now found themselves. Ultimately, however, they would be defeated and Cambronne taken prisoner. The emperor's final throw of the dice had failed.

FINAL ACTIONS AT HOUGOUMONT

Back at Hougoumont the French attacks had continued between the setting alight of some of the buildings and the attack of the Garde Impériale. There was some confusion regarding who was in overall command of the defence and, although Hepburn was now acting brigade commander following the wounding of Sir George Cooke, it appears Lieutenant-Colonel Francis Home of the 2/3rd Guards had believed he was the most senior officer in Hougoumont.

Between 15:30 and 19:00 the French had mounted a number of attacks into the orchard, which were then subject to counter-attacks by the defenders. These attacks eventually started to slow as the troops involved in the struggle for Hougoumont began to tire. The French had failed to take the château, but the defenders were hanging on by their fingernails. However, about thirty minutes before the Garde Impériale began their final advance, the defenders were reinforced by the late Ompteda's 2nd KGL Brigade, Major von Hammerstein's Hanovarian Salzgitter Landwehr Battalion and the Advantgarde, Leib and 1st Light Battalions from Olfermann's Brunswick division. These troops moved into the orchard and drove away any remaining French soldiers.

During the defence of Hougoumont, Wellington had committed a total of 6,000 men at one point or another during the day. The French had likewise committed between 8,000 and 9,000 in their repeated attacks, troops that the emperor could ill afford to spare given the arrival of the Prussians. It is worth ending the description of the struggle for Hougoumont by noting the considerable effort made by the German troops, who doggedly stood side by side with their British guardsmen counterparts throughout the battle.

THE FALL OF PLANCENOIT

As the attack of the Garde Impériale began to fail, Blücher was preparing his own final assault, this time one that would take Plancenoit and completely drive out the French defenders. The assault was led by the 5th Brigade of Pirch's II Corps, while to the north of the village Bülow's 13th and 15th brigades launched an assault against Lobau. Supporting these leading formations were the 14th and 16th brigades, also of Bülow's IV Corps. In all, some 24,000 Prussian troops were involved in the final push to take Plancenoit.

The attack began at 20:00, with Major von Roebel's 5th Westphalian Landwehr deploying to the north; Major von Cardell's 2nd Regiment driving into the centre towards the village square and church; and Major von Helmenstreit's 25th Regiment bypassing it to the south. For the next thirty minutes the village again became the scene of bitter street and house fighting, but eventually the Prussians were able to virtually surround the village. Realising their situation to be impossible, the French began to withdraw under cover of Captain Peschot's company of 1/2e Chasseurs. Plancenoit was finally in Prussian hands.

THE FRENCH ARMY DISINTEGRATES

The sight of the Garde Impériale withdrawing caused unsteadiness among many of the French troops along Napoleon's line in this section of the battlefield. However, it was probably the panic among the men of Durutte's 4th Infantry Division, who were retiring in the face of the superior numbers of Zieten's I Corps, which sparked the disintegration of the French army. This panic rippled along the French line and reached the emperor's centre left about the same time as the repulse of the Garde Impériale.

A sense of defeat was beginning to prevail over the French army, and it was now that Wellington ordered a general advance. As the men of the Anglo-Allied army moved off, cheers erupted along the line, although the advance was conducted in a somewhat disorderly manner. Most of the duke's men were by now exhausted and few managed to move forward more than a few hundred yards.

However, much of the Anglo-Allied light cavalry had played little or no role in the battle so far, and as such these men were still relatively fresh. Vivian pressed Wellington for permission to charge, and as the duke consented Uxbridge asked to lead the advance himself. Unfortunately, it was at this moment that a fragment from a cannon shell shattered the earl's leg. As the injured Uxbridge was taken to the rear, Vivian led his light cavalry brigade forward and began to exert pressure on the retreating Old Guard. Meanwhile, Vandeleur's brigade began to harass Reille's II Corps, which eventually broke and fled.

Following the capture of Plancenoit, the Prussians were now also advancing towards La Belle Alliance. With that, the two battalions of the 1er Grenadiers

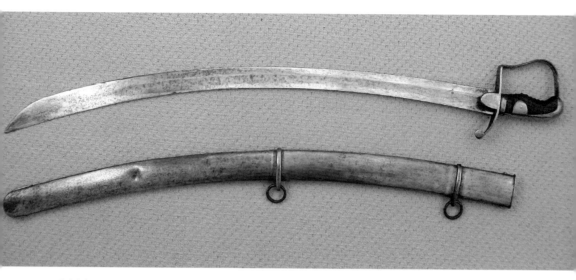

British 1796 Pattern Light Cavalry Sabre carried by Hussars and Light Dragoons. (Author's collection)

A defeated Napoleon sits mounted inside the protection of a square formed by his Old Guard. (Andrew Field)

à Pied (the 'Oldest of the Old'), under Maréchal de Camp Jean-Martin Petit, formed two defensive squares. Initially Napoleon had been placed in one of these squares for protection, but he soon left on horseback for Le Caillou, from where he departed the field to head back to France under the protection of the 1/1er Chasseurs. The battle was now all but over and the emperor had lost.

Wellington and Blücher finally met at La Belle Alliance around 21:00. As they did so the Prussian was said to have leaned over from his saddle to embrace and then kiss the duke, something which Wellington was noted as being visibly uncomfortable with. The two then conversed over what to do next, and it was decided that the Prussians should pursue both Napoleon and his routed army.

The meeting of Wellington and Blücher at La Belle Alliance. It would be here that Blücher would throw his arms around Wellington and kiss him, much to the latter's discomfort. (Anne S. K. Brown Military Collection, Brown University Library)

8
AFTERMATH

THE PRUSSIAN PURSUIT

The Prussian pursuit of the defeated French army was to be a vicious one. Indeed, when Prussian troops arrived at Le Caillou they set fire to the buildings, burning alive the wounded French soldiers inside. Napoleon, meanwhile, had caught up with his personal baggage train, including his campaign carriage, which had been sent back towards France by his valet in an attempt to save the gold, banknotes and other treasures belonging to the emperor. Unfortunately for Napoleon the route was clogged by his fleeing soldiers, transport wagons and horses, with everything moving at a painfully slow pace.

Some distance behind the emperor, the Prussian advance left a trail of death and destruction. Wounded or straggling French soldiers, officers and men alike, were bayoneted and robbed of anything deemed of value. So ferocious was the pursuit that Lieutenant Jackson, who was on Wellington's staff and who had advanced further than most in the Anglo-Allied army, felt threatened by his Prussian allies when he found himself among them. So much so he drew a hasty retreat and was relieved to see the red-coated infantrymen of the 52nd Foot.

An increasingly desperate French army began to shed any encumbrances in an attempt to aid escape. Guns and wagons were abandoned, which would be scooped up by the advancing Prussians as war booty. It has been argued that the realisation of the spoils of war is what spurred on many of the exhausted Prussian troops. Indeed, during the pursuit a Major von Keller of the 15th Prussian Infantry Regiment acquired Napoleon's sword, medals, diamonds and hat, which were found in his captured carriage.

Although the French army was now in a rout from the battlefield, it should be noted that several French units did in fact manage to stay relatively intact and conduct an orderly withdrawal to safety. Some of these units even escorted with them Allied prisoners of war, many of which were to remain in captivity for several weeks after the battle.

Prussian cavalry charging a body of French fugitives on the road to Genappe. The Prussian pursuit of the broken French army would be vicious and little quarter was shown. (Anne S. K. Brown Military Collection, Brown University Library)

THE BATTLE OF WAVRE

Although the Battle of Waterloo was practically over, the Battle of Wavre, fought between Grouchy's force and Thielmann's Prussian III Corps, was still raging. As previously noted, the battle began about 16:00, when General Vandamme's French III Corps came into contact with Prussian outposts to the east of the town. The French pushed these Prussian troops back before launching their main assault on Wavre. However, the Prussians held their ground and several attacks by the French to seize crossings over the Dyle River failed. The first of these assaults was led by Gérard, who was seriously wounded at Bierges, south-west of Wavre, while the second was led by Grouchy himself.

After these failed attempts, Grouchy decided to send Général de Division Pierre Claude Pajol's I Cavalry Corps and François Antoine Teste's 21st Infantry Division to the nearby hamlet of Limale to seize the crossing there. Limale was quickly captured at 19:00 and so was the crossing at the hamlet of

Limelette. Grouchy then ordered divisions of Gérard's Corps, which had just arrived, to proceed to reinforce Pajol and Teste. Thielmann counter-attacked, but by 23:00 the French had beaten him off. As the day came to an end the battle appeared to be in a state of stalemate but Grouchy, unaware the emperor had been defeated at Waterloo, intended to renew his attack in the morning.

The battle resumed hours later, and eventually Grouchy could claim victory over the Prussians at about 10:00. However, about half an hour later news arrived of the Allied victory at Waterloo, rendering the French victory at Wavre meaningless. Thus ended the last major action of the Waterloo campaign of 1815, although a few more minor skirmishes would take place until the Allies finally occupied Paris less than two weeks later.

THE DEAD AND WOUNDED

Casualty figures for Waterloo are estimated to have been around 15,000 for the Anglo-Allied army and 7,000 for the Prussian army. Calculating French losses, however, is extremely difficult and suggested figures have ranged from under 22,000 to over 31,000. While such numbers may sound staggering today, we must remember they were comparatively light in the context of Napoleonic battles. Indeed, at the Battle of Leipzig, fought in October 1813, some 92,000 were killed or wounded. Perhaps the most remarkable aspect related to Waterloo casualties is the fact that so many occurred in such a small area. Again, if we compare Waterloo to Leipzig, the former was fought over a two-mile front while the later stretched for twenty-one miles. As such, the slaughter of 18 June 1815 appears to have been intensive within a confined area.

As one might expect, the daylight of the morning after the battle revealed an awful sight. Thousands of dead and dying were stretched out across the ground so viciously contested only hours before, and those lucky enough, or perhaps unlucky enough, to have survived their wounds had to contend with the local peasantry. The local inhabitants spent much of the night and following days scavenging the field for anything of value, including the boots or clothes of the dead or dying men, weapons, money, pocket watches, or just about anything they considered of value. Even days or weeks after the battle, corpses would be robbed of their teeth, which were later used in the production of false dentures.

The field of Waterloo as it appeared the morning after the battle. The ground was littered with the dead and dying, with many of the latter lying where they fell for days. (Anne S. K. Brown Military Collection, Brown University Library)

Nor was it just human suffering that occupied the field in the wake of the fighting. The horses had also been subjected to the same shot and shell as the soldiers. Many were seen in a terrible state, some still alive with their innards hanging out or back legs shot away. Reading eyewitness accounts of the days after the battle often reveals how the soldiers, even battle-hardened veterans, found the suffering of the animals harder to bear than those of their fellow men. Wounded horses who were lucky would be found by a soldier or officer who would put them out of their misery with a shot to the head.

Parties of uninjured soldiers were sent out to collect the wounded and move them to areas where they could be loaded on to transports bound for one of the improvised hospitals. The work was long and hard, with many of the wounded having to spend days lying helpless where they fell, until they were either found or simply died. The French soldiers had the worst of it, often being left to last, and it was not unknown for them to call out to their enemies, begging to be shot. Even those fortunate enough to have arrived at one of the hospitals, which were spread out across Brussels and elsewhere, could hope for little better, facing amputations, infections and more death.

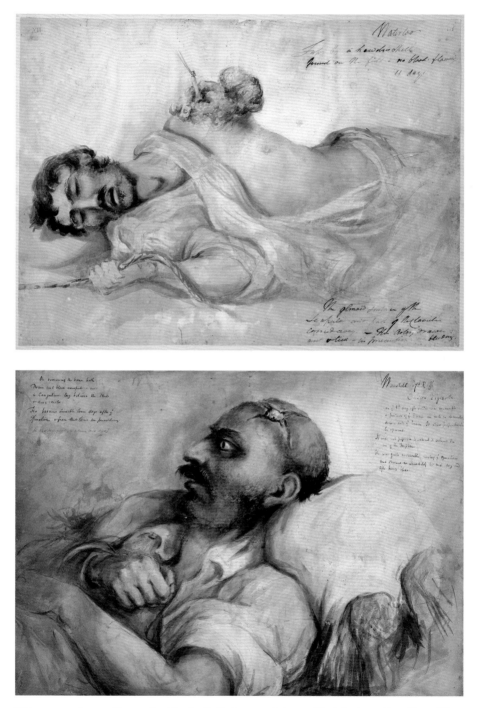

This page and next: Pictures by Charles Bell of some of the terrible injuries suffered by soldiers during the Battle of Waterloo. (Wellcome Library, London)

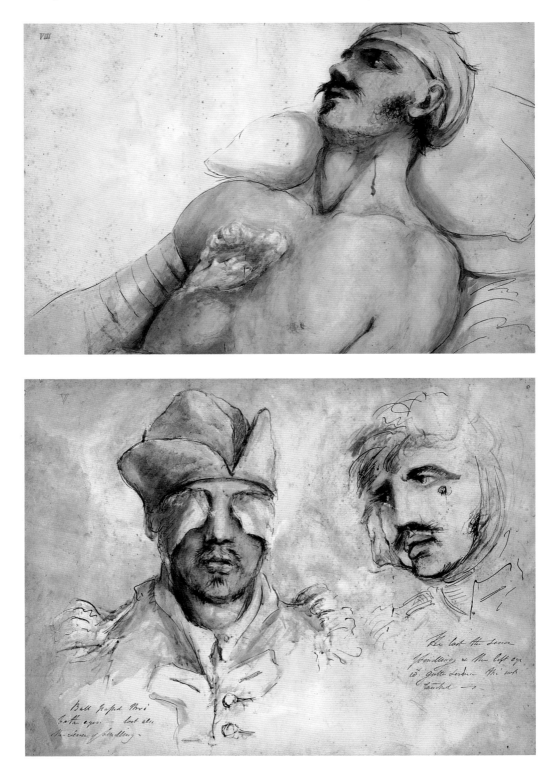

NAPOLEON'S SECOND ABDICATION AND EXILE TO SAINT HELENA

Napoleon arrived back in Paris having escaped the Prussian pursuit, but he found that the people of France had turned against him. He had little choice but to abdicate for a second time, which he did on 22 June in the somewhat foolish hope that his son would be allowed to take over as emperor. With that he left Paris for Malmaison, but as Allied troops travelled further into the French interior he planned to journey to Rochfort, from where he hoped to flee to the United States. However, the British Royal Navy appeared to be one step ahead of the former emperor, and were blockading the port.

Eventually Napoleon surrendered to the British, who placed him aboard HMS *Bellerophon* on 15 July for transportation to England. It would be the British that the former emperor now pinned his hopes on for a future life, but in the end it was decided he would again be sent into exile, this time to the more remote island of Saint Helena in the Atlantic Ocean. Although several plots to rescue him from exile were considered by various people, none came to anything, and it would be on Saint Helena that Napoleon Bonaparte would die on 5 May 1821, aged fifty-one years.

To this day we do not really know for sure the cause of Napoleon's death, although stomach cancer was stated as the reason at the time. Much later it was suggested that he had in fact been poisoned, which some scientists have attempted to prove through the testing of surviving hair samples. Even more recently other scientists have suggested the evidence actually points to the fact he did indeed have stomach cancer. We do know, however, that the emperor's health had been failing for some time before the Battle of Waterloo, and some of his supporters have used this as evidence of his lack of performance. While this is again another debated aspect of the Waterloo legend, it is probably reasonable to assume he was suffering poor health on 18 June 1815.

THE BATTLEFIELD TODAY

Today the Battlefield of Waterloo has become a major tourist attraction, and the fascination with both Napoleon and the battle appears to be stronger than ever. Although an ever-expanding Brussels has encroached on the site, it remains relatively intact, with the buildings at Hougoumont, La Haye-Sainte, La Belle Alliance and Le Caillou still standing. The latter, where the emperor set up his headquarters, is now a museum and holds various items from the period, including Napoleon's camp bed, the table upon which he spread his maps and his funeral mask.

One curious feature of the battlefield today that did not exist on 18 June 1815 is the so-called Lion Mound erected in the 1820s by King William I of the Netherlands to mark the spot where his son, the Prince of Orange-Nassau, was wounded during the battle. As the name suggests, there is a large lion statue on the top of the forty-metre-high mound, and those who fancy the climb can walk up the steps to the top, from where they can experience a fantastic view of the battlefield. There is also a panoramic table informing the visitor where the various units were at different stages of the battle.

Also of interest to the visitor is the Wellington Museum located in the village of Waterloo itself. This building is in fact the coaching inn where the duke located his headquarters before the battle, and from where he wrote his famous despatch afterwards. The inn was converted into a museum in 1955 and today holds a

The south gate at Hougoumont in 2011 prior to the recent restoration work. (Photo by Andrew Browning)

number of original artefacts from the battle. Visitors can also take a look at the rooms where Wellington stayed, as well as those of his aide-de-camp, Colonel Gordon. The gravestones of some of Wellington's men are in the garden of the museum, but the Waterloo roads were widened in the intervening years and their graves have sadly been lost.

With the approach of the 200th anniversary of the battle, a great deal of effort has gone into preserving the battle site, including an extensive restoration project of the Hougoumont château. Other areas of the battlefield have also benefited from repair and restoration work, particularly a number of memorials located around the site. Restoration work to the frontage of the Mont-Saint-Jean farm has been carried out and two old hotels, built after the battle, have been demolished as part of the major revamp.

Finally, it is most certainly worth mentioning that the battlefield hosts a number of re-enactment events, where the visitor is treated to a wonderful spectacle of Napoleonic uniforms and equipment representing all nationalities involved. While the horrors of the fighting can never be truly understood by those of us looking back from the safe distance of 200 years, the onlooker is able to take a small glimpse into what it may have been like on that historic day in 1815.

The memorial plaque commemorating the part played by the Coldstream Guards at Hougoumont. (Photo by Andrew Browning)

WHAT NEXT?

FURTHER READING

Adkin, Mark, *The Waterloo Companion: The Complete Guide to History's Most Famous Land Battle* (London: Aurum, 2001)

Barbero, Alessandro, *The Battle: A History of the Battle of Waterloo* (London: Atlantic Books, 2006)

Clayton, Tim, *Waterloo: Four Days That Changed Europe's Destiny* (London: Little, Brown, 2014)

Field, Andrew W., *Waterloo: The French Perspective* (Barnsley: Pen & Sword, 2012)

Franklin, John, *Waterloo 1815 (1): Quatre Bras* (Oxford: Osprey, 2014)

Franklin, John, *Waterloo 1815 (2): Ligny* (Oxford: Osprey, 2015)

Fremont-Barnes, Gregory, *The French Revolutionary Wars* (Oxford: Osprey, 2001)

Fremont-Barnes, Gregory, *Waterloo 1815: The British Army's Day of Destiny* (Stroud: The History Press, 2014)

Hibbert, Christopher, *The French Revolution* (London: Penguin, 1982)

Hofschröer, Peter, *Waterloo 1815: Wavre to Plancenoit* (Barnsley: Pen & Sword, 2013)

Holmes, Richard, *Wellington: The Iron Duke* (London: Harper Collins, 2003)

Leggiere, Michael V., *Blücher: Scourge of Napoleon* (Norman: University of Oklahoma Press, 2014)

McLynn, Frank, *Napoleon: A Biography* (London: Pimlico, 1998)

O'Keeffe, Paul, *Waterloo: The Aftermath* (London: The Bodley Head, 2014)

WEBSITES OF INTEREST

Napoleonic Wars Forum: http://www.napoleonicwarsforum.com

The Napoleon Series: http://www.napoleon-series.org

The Waterloo Association: http://waterlooassociation.org.uk

Waterloo 200: http://www.waterloo200.org

Waterloo Battlefield (official site for visitors): http://www.waterloo1815.be

FILM AND TV DOCUMENTARIES

The Waterloo Collection Parts 1 to 4, 2011. [DVD] (Battlefield History TV/Pen & Sword)

Waterloo, 1970. [Film] Directed by Sergey Bondarchuk (Universal Pictures)

INDEX

Also in the Illustrated Introductions series

Fascinated by history? Wish you knew more?
The Illustrated Introductions are here to help.

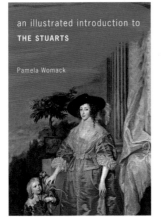

An Illustrated Introduction
to the Stuarts

978-1-4456-3788-4
£9.99

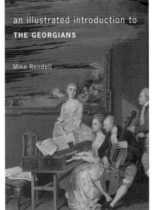

An Illustrated Introduction
to the Georgians

978-1-4456-3630-6
£9.99

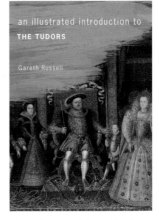

An Illustrated Introduction
to the Tudors

978-1-4456-4121-8
£9.99

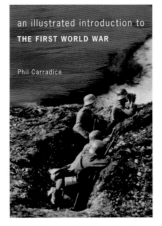

An Illustrated Introduction
to the First World War

978-1-4456-3296-4
£9.99

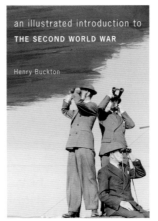

An Illustrated Introduction
to the Second World War

978-1-4456-3848-5
£9.99

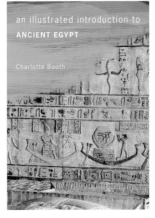

An Illustrated Introduction
to Ancient Egypt

978-1-4456-3365-7
£9.99

Available from all good bookshops or to order direct
Please call **01453-847-800**
www.amberley-books.com